MW01015772

It's a Whale of a Tale

by

Nadine Thomas Maclean

To Jim & Caroline:

I am so thrilled to share my memories with you two. Thank you for asking.

Nadine MacLean

DORRANCE PUBLISHING CO., INC.
PITTSBURGH, PENNSYLVANIA 15222

All Rights Reserved
Copyright © 1999 by Nadine Thomas MacLean
No part of this book may be reproduced or transmitted
in any form or by any means, electronic or mechanical,
including photocopying, recording, or by any information
storage and retrieval system without permission in
writing from the publisher.

ISBN # 0-8059-4467-2
Printed in the United States of America

First Printing

For information or to order additional books, please write:
Dorrance Publishing Co., Inc.
643 Smithfield Street
Pittsburgh, Pennsylvania 15222
U.S.A.

In memory of Aunt Florence and Uncle Chet because they cared.

Contents

Chapter One

My story begins with my grandparents, Robert and Cynthia Henkle. They were responsible for giving me a mother I cherished with all my heart. Her name was Esther, a small, shy lady with reddish-brown hair. "Oh, she is the lady with the lovely hands," her friends would say. They not only were the most beautiful hands I had known, but the most comforting.

My grandparents were accountable for my exquisite place of birth because of their strong minds and bodies which brought them over the Oregon Trail to the Willamette Valley of Oregon. They must have been overwhelmed with the brilliant array of green, rolling hills, framed by majestic snowcapped mountains, so this is where they settled. I say, "Thank you." They gave me a home of beauty February 3, 1921. This is where my life and story begins as Thia Nadine Thomas.

My Welsh father, Fred Thomas, came to Oregon after serving in World War I with a dream of becoming a medical doctor. He did not realize that he would fall in love with my mother and marry. Nor did he imagine that ten months later I would be born. His becoming a doctor was given up because he lacked financial funds, but he was so rich when it came to artistic talents. He was a very sensitive man, but one who loved to laugh. I thought he was the most handsome, smartest man alive. He was tall with gorgeous, dark, wavy hair, and gray eyes. My parents made an attractive couple even though they were very poor with nothing to call their own.

My mother had two brothers who were successful morticians, Chester and Roy Henkle, and since my father was medically inclined he followed in their footsteps. When he became a licensed mortician, we moved to Sheridan, Oregon, a delightful small town. He bought a funeral home there and became prosperous. My memories of those years were happy ones. Even though I was not a healthy child, I must have been a happy one because happiness is all I remember. I love thinking about our happy home in Sheridan. It was a comfortable house—gray with white trim—and it seemed as though my mother had tons of flowers, especially larkspur and clarkia. I remember the fun times pulling my wagon on the wooden sidewalk in front of our house and the clicking sound the wheels made. The faster I went, the louder the clicks.

How wonderful to have the Yamhill River below our house. Every summer afternoon my mother and father would take me swimming. I don't remember never being able to swim. My mother said, "Nadine swam before she walked. She would hold tight to her father's neck as he swam out into the deepest part of the river." It must have been a real breathtaking experience for me. I loved it, it made me laugh. My mother, however, did not enjoy this activity. It made her feel a little frantic inside.

My first baby picture was taken of me while I sat naked in the Yamhill River. I would be so embarrassed for people to see it, even though I was only a few months old.

It was July of 1925 when my sister Sylvia was born. She was a beautiful baby with lovely, blonde curly hair and pretty blue eyes. I can't say I was ever jealous of her, but I did have hurt feelings when our friends would ooh and aah over Sylvia's gorgeous blonde hair and ignore me completely. I was referred to as "the puny one." Mother was very aware of this, so one afternoon she brushed and brushed my straight hair and then said excitedly, "You know, I can see my face in your hair, it is like a mirror. You are so special." Bless her, I did feel special, so whenever I would be called puny, I would think, They don't know what they are talking about, because I knew I was special without the lemon juice on my hair. All that I needed was my mother's hairbrush and her kind words. How wise she was.

Our home was filled with music. If mother wasn't playing the piano, my dad, being the typical Welshman that he was, would make music from his saxophone; harpsichord; or my favorite, the harmonica. Music was a big part of my childhood. My talent was singing. Mother recognized this so she worked with me almost every day. I learned and memorized many songs. Mother saw to it that I would sing for special occasions. There was one song that my mother was especially pleased with called *"I'm Daddy's Sweetheart."* She was so elated with this number that she made arrangements for me to sing it on a radio show, *"Stars of Tomorrow,"* in Portland, Oregon. There was much excitement over this adventure. Of course, my mother was thrilled beyond words, but I was too young to be in much of a dither—I was happier over my new fancy dress! However, the trip to Portland was not to be. My father had a phone call just as we were ready to leave: someone had passed away. Mother was crushed and in tears. "People always die at the wrong time," she sobbed. Of course, she didn't mean to say those words. Needless to say, there are many drawbacks about being a mortician. It hurt me to see my mother cry, but we do recover from life's disappointments. Our happy home continued with as much music as ever. Even at bedtime, Dad made sounds like a trumpet through an old phonograph megaphone for Sylvia and me to march up the stairs and into bed.

Yes, we were two fortunate young girls to have the parents we had. They gave us the best of everything. Moral values were as important to them as our ABC's, and I am grateful for that. I did have my favorite times, especially going shopping with Mother, which always was during the afternoon. She made sure that we were spic and span and that our dresses were fresh and clean—Sylvia in blue, and I would be in pink. Mother always wore a pretty hat and high heels, and she carried a delightful shopping basket. If it happened to be a hot afternoon, she would use a parasol to protect her face from the sun's rays. Then she would remind us to use our tiny parasols. It was such a fun experience going to the meatmarket, and if we had been good during the week, the butcher would give us a free hotdog. Believe me, those hotdogs could never be duplicated. If Mother was in an especially good mood, she would treat us to ice cream at the drugstore soda fountain. The ice cream was special, but it was the delectable fragrance of the drugstore and the very high soda fountain chairs that I so fondly remember. Sheridan was a small, friendly town. Mother enjoyed these treasured afternoons just to visit with her many dear friends during these shopping trips. Yes, it was an important part of her day.

Mischievous! Yes, we were. Sylvia took the scissors to the cat's whiskers, so I gave Sylvia a little trim. Mother had a fit of sorts. Of course, mainly because of Sylvia's hair. Another incident that horrified those who knew us was the day I fell into a barrel of tar that was out front of the creamery. I thought the tar would taste like Black Jack gum. I did, however, have a good chew.

There was one memorable summer afternoon when my girlfriend and I decided to become two dancing cupids, just like the naked cupids which were in the center of my friend's fish pond. The Yamhill River was the dividing line between the neighborhood and the business district of Sheridan, so my friend and I were entertaining the citizens of Sheridan, including my father. I spent the rest of the day with a red bottom, and most of all, hurt feelings.

We were the same as most kids and were in awe of persons who were different. This was the way I felt about a Mennonite family living across the street from us. I was fascinated with them. The lady always wore long, black dresses and a black bonnet. The husband also wore black. They didn't believe in any modern conveniences, including electricity. At night I could see the light of an oil lamp, so strange and so spooky. I wondered what they would do if I stole rhubarb from their garden, so I did just that. They didn't do anything about it, but that was no sign my mother didn't. I ate raw rhubarb for lunch while the family had pie. I learned that day that it is everyone's right to be the way they wish to be.

One very warm fall day, just before our noon meal, my father decided to clean his rifle. He and his buddies were to leave soon on a hunting trip, so this was part of the preparation. "Not in the kitchen," protested my mother, but her words landed on deaf ears. Before any of us knew what was going on, Dad's rifle accidentally discharged and Mother threw her teakettle at the same time. How fortunate we were that the only damage done was to the kitchen window. The blast brought our neighbors scurrying to our house, only to find my dad doubled up in laughter and Mother in a fit of rage. The smell of gunpowder lingered in the air and our memories. Bedtime was different that night. Dad slept upstairs and Mother occupied the guestroom. This different procedure surely did impress me because my parents never quarreled. Not in front of us, anyway. There was only one other time, when Dad gave my mother a driving lesson. She came home in tears and Dad did not speak to anyone! We were happy to have a home without bickering and disagreements.

Chapter Two

I couldn't have been more than five years old, but I well remember when we went to the big city of Portland for a few days. The main reason for the trip was for me to be checked over by Dr. Builderback, a well-known pediatrician. I must have been in good health because the next few days were spent taking in the sights of Portland. The big attraction for me was the elaborate vaudeville at the gorgeous Paramount Theater. I was spellbound with the beautiful show girls. I had never seen anything like it before—the brilliant colors of their costumes; feathers; jewelry; and, above all, the dancing and music. I could have stayed there forever.

It was very exciting to come to the city, not just for me but for Mother and Dad as well. Just walking down Broadway was a thrill and to watch taffy being made in the popular candy shop was an eye-popping experience for me. I think I must have been hypnotized because I thought this would be a nice place to stay. Of course, we didn't leave without a box of candy.

We spent the night at the Portland Hotel and had dinner there. The dining room was sophisticated and luxurious. I was given behavior instructions: I should have the best of manners so as not to embarrass anyone. What Mother and Dad didn't count on was that the waiters were all black. This was the first time I had ever seen a black person. I did just fine until our waiter tied a knot at one end of my napkin and stuck it down in front of the neck of my dress. I cried, and my folks were embarrassed after all. I didn't get lectured until we were back in our room. Then and there I learned a little about black people, as I did about the Mennonites.

The four of us had wonderful holidays, and birthdays were always special. Christmas and Thanksgiving Day were spent with my mother's relatives. Mother came from a big family, and each brother and sister was delightful in his or her own way. My grandmother Cynthia had always been a favorite love of my life. She was quite a composed and unruffled lady. She made me feel content and peaceful while near her. I could say anything that I wanted to and she would not scold or correct me. Only "That's all right, honeybun," she would softly say. I was proud to have been named Thia, short for her beautiful name Cynthia. I knew that she loved me, as I loved her. I so often wondered why she had so many heartaches, one right after another. Her daughter Mamie passed away just before I was born. I wished many times that I could have known her. It was said that I was an exact copy of her. Grandmother also had a baby girl die, and of course her beloved husband passed on following the death of Mamie. Why should my lovely grandmother have had so much sorrow? Her youngest son, Herman, had a devastating fall from the second story of their farmhouse. He was but four years old. Even though he became a physically healthy grown man, his mind did not develop past his four years of age. This was another devastating tragedy which brought out my grandmother's emotional courage and bravery. I hope she did cry during her quiet times.

Ora was my mother's oldest sister. She was a caring person with a sunny personality, loving a good laugh (or maybe a chuckle would do). Now, all of the Henkles were marvelous cooks and expert gardeners. If prizes were given for such, I am sure Ora would have won a blue ribbon in both categories. At one time she owned a restaurant in Tillamook, Oregon, called "Frenchies." She was a cute, short, plump little lady with a glorious, jolly personality! She married Uncle Kile late in life and they made their home in Garibaldi, Oregon, which was near Tillamook. He was a kind, pleasant man who adored his pipe. He always had pennies and a stick of gum in his pocket for Sylvia and me, so very soon he became a favorite for both of us. Everyone who knew this tall, thin man liked and respected him.

My uncle Roy would be considered the character of Tillamook, I am sure. He was a mortician and the coroner of Tillamook County. He was a small man with very dark, straight hair. I never did see him angry. I am sure that he thought showing anger was a waste of time. Of course, I will admit, he enjoyed the effects of liquor. Being a youngster, I, of course, thought of him as just being so much fun! He enjoyed telling stories, but you would have to have plenty of spare time to ever hear the ending of his yarns. Often I would forget what the story was about in the first place. He was a delight. Yes, a small man, but he had a heart as big as a mountain. Everyone in Tillamook loved him. His first wife passed away, leaving him with a daughter, Ellna, and a son, Willis. Uncle Roy remarried a woman called Jessie, so Ellna and Willis had a stepmother. She was a big woman—not fat, just a big woman with many artistic talents. Everything she did was perfect except housekeeping. I remember hearing the concerns from my mother and father's conversations as to how strict she was, especially with Willis. I felt nervous whenever I was around her, and yet she made and gave me so many of my favorite dresses. And, in spite of her overbearing and bossy personality, she had a terrific sense of humor.

Ada was the second sister of my mother's and she, too, lived in Tillamook. Her husband, Uncle Frank, was a builder and a cabinetmaker.

They also owned an apartment complex next to their home. They were a hard-working couple, but they always had time for wonderful trips and fabulous parties. I believe they belonged to every organization in Tillamook. Whenever I think of beautiful lawns and flowers, my thoughts turn to Aunt Ada. Her landscape was an exquisite view of skilled gardening. It reminded me of a beautiful park. It was never unusual for tourists to stop long enough to take a picture. Aunt Ada was a fun person, but believe me, she did have a temper. She made up for Uncle Roy's lackadaisical manner. God help a dog that would stray close to her well-groomed lawn. She would never hesitate to use her BB gun. She was also a fantastic gourmet cook, as well as being an excellent seamstress. Uncle Frank was a well-educated, well-respected man and one of the best contractors in Tillamook County. He wasn't handsome at all. He was bald and had a big belly. I though of him as being odd because of the weird high-up shoes he wore. Mother would get after me to be nicer to him; after all, he had made a delightful cupboard and table for my doll dishes. I tried to become more cordial but couldn't help feeling uncomfortable and skittish whenever he came near me.

Uncle Chester, Mother's other brother, was completely opposite from Uncle Roy. He was a big man with strong features. He commanded respect with a glint in his eye. He took pride in everything that he did, or he wouldn't do it at all. He was a successful businessman. Yes, he also was a mortician and coroner of his county, as well as a noteworthy banker. His wife, Florence, felt it was very special—and it most assuredly was—that many prominent investors would seek his advice. He was very fond of football since he played ball for the Willamette University during the early 1900s. He was a tackle for their team, but when Oregon State College needed a fullback they called on my uncle. Yes, things were very different in those days. Uncle Chet, as I called him, was as polished and extremely orderly about himself as he was about his business. However, he, too, enjoyed his liquor. Then things would become comical or even embarrassing.

Aunt Florence was what I call a perfect lady, proper in every way. Her parents left her quite a large sum of money, so it was she who built their beautiful home in Dallas, Oregon, another charming Willamette Valley town. I would say that their home was the most elegant house in Dallas at that time. She was very kind to everyone regardless of who or what they were. I can't remember her ever speaking ill of anyone. It was easy for everyone to love her. Yes, she was a lady in every way but that didn't mean she couldn't appreciate a good joke. She loved to put forth a hardy laugh. Their home was impressive, but it was her artistic talents, expressed throughout the house, that made it an endearing home.

My grandmother lived next door to them in Dallas. It was Uncle Chet and Aunt Florence who looked after Grandmother. It was these two wonderful people who made certain that Herman was cared for in a state hospital for the mentally ill. Grandmother would have him for a week or two during the summer and Uncle Chet would often bring him home for Christmas as well.

Christmas and Thanksgiving were two of our special holidays. Not just for the elegant dinners or the many Christmas gifts, but it was being with all the aunts, uncles, and cousins, and the thrill I felt being near my grandmother. I loved to touch her. What a joyous time it was for all of us, so much laughter and fun. Ellna and Willis were special too. They both were several years older than me, but I didn't care. I still liked to be with them. Ellna would giggle every time I did something, regardless of what it was, so I had a blast performing. It was just silly stuff. I'm sure Willis was bored, but I still found it fun to show off in front of him whether he laughed or not!

Decoration Day, which we now call Memorial Day, was a very important event for our family. Aunt Ada and Aunt Jessie would venture up into the coast range and gather wild rhododendron blooms, filling box after box for our cemetery. Mother and Grandmother would take flowers from their yard. Every Memorial Day was special, but there is one that stands out in my mind above all the rest. It was a gorgeous, clear day, except for a few fluffy white clouds. It was fun to drive up the old cemetery hill and watch the rolling, white clouds. Some of them resembled dogs, cats, and even elephants. To my amazement, a beautiful angel appeared. I was overwhelmed. She seemed to be hovering over the cemetery. She must have really loved our people, and now I understood why our relatives are buried so high up on this hill: They are closer to the angels and to heaven! We were never to disturb Dad while he was driving, but I said it anyway. "I know why Grandpa and his children are buried up high on this hill. It is because they are close to heaven and the angels." Mother and Father didn't have a word to say, there was only silence until we arrived. Then Mother and Father both hugged me. Mother said, "You are a dear child." This has been a cherished, unforgettable memory.

My aunts, uncles, and grandmother were already there, busy with their flowers and the picnic dinner. My uncles were having a great time visiting with old friends and fetching water for the flower containers. Grandmother watched her family from the shade of the old maple tree. It was a delightful time. The cousins were both there. Willis was bored unless he could tease one of us, but Ellna was tickled to be with us. This was her "giggle time." How I did enjoy thinking up things that would strike her funny bone.

The old Philomath Cemetery is a beautiful place with wild pink roses overflowing the old cemetery fence. The abundant supply of wild strawberries was very much a pleasing sight, especially for children. When I thought that no one was watching, I would place a wild rose on each grave and say, "Now, this is from me." After the graves were all decorated, it would be time for our picnic, which I always called "a picnic spread." Our tablecloths were placed on the ground under Grandma's maple tree. There was an abundance of food, but it all was very gourmet as well. Grandmother never failed to bring her dried apricot pie and a loaf of salt-risen bread.

Before the day was over, I felt I must tell Ellna and Willis about why our cemetery was so high up on the hill. "Bet you don't know why the cemetery is so high up in the sky!" I shouted. I knew that they didn't know. "It is because it is closer to heaven and to the angels." Ellna burst into a fit of giggles and Willis just shook his head and said, "You just get dumber and dumber." Of course, I was crushed for a minute or two. Then I thought, *I will get even with Willis and tell him that it is safe now to use the old outhouse and the bad smell is gone.* Sure enough, he believed me. He did go into the stinky outhouse, and he left it as if he had been shot. Ellna went into uncontrollable hee-haws. I wanted to hide, but I didn't. Willis shouted, "I'll get even, stupid."

"You just don't know that I am a dear child," I reminded him.

Our graves were all decorated and, according to Aunt Ada, they were the most beautiful in the cemetery. Everyone agreed that our picnic dinners only became better each year. We were all packed up, ready to leave for home, except Uncle Chet. As usual, he still was visiting with old friends—friends that he grew up with, friends whose parents came over the Oregon Trail together. "We must all be patient with him," Mother reminded us as she fussed about the strawberry stains on our dresses.

Chapter Three

I was eight years old when my father chose to go into business with Uncle Chet in Dallas, Oregon. Leaving our cherished home and so many dear friends was difficult, especially for Mother. This move of ours caused many changes for all members of our family. First of all, my grandmother had to give up her home so that we could move into her house. She settled into a smaller place, just behind our house. Uncle Chet and Aunt Florence lived next door. The mortuary was in the same block, as were the garages for the family cars. All of this was too much togetherness...too much for Mother. However, she did wonders with Grandmother's house. It was marvelous how she made a charming room for Sylvia and me by converting a screened back porch. I was thrilled with it because it was pink and big enough to be a playroom. There was a porch which went around the house with a railing. Sylvia and I enjoyed it, especially on rainy days, but Mother did not. She would say how dark and gloomy it made the house. Mother, I am sure, was not too happy. She was bound to miss all of her close friends, and I doubt very much if she enjoyed living close to her brother, even though she loved him.

There was an unfortunate incident the afternoon she drove into the side of the garage. Uncle Chet literally came unglued. He really lost his temper with Mother, and of course, this upset Dad. He became angry with Uncle Chet for jumping all over Mother. He was, however, put out with Mother for being so careless about her driving. Well, they all lived through this upset. Bless Grandma, she always stayed clear of any disagreements.

Our family was becoming more accustomed to our new home and new friends, though Mother would complain as to how dark the house was. "The porch seems to cut the light from view," she would say. She was trying to adjust, but in the back of her mind, she was lonely for her Sheridan home and friends. My father did promise her a new home in the near future, so this brought about exciting plans for her to think about.

The citizens of Dallas had much pride in their town. The streets were always clean and the buildings well cared for. Everyone would be enthusiastic and eager for new improvements in their town. Everyone that I knew would rave about our city park's swimming pool, which was a dammed-up river. I become excited about it, even as I think of it today. It was cold! But the greatest swimming in the world!

The Polk County Courthouse occupied the center of Dallas. It was a beautiful, gray, stone building with a high clock tower. Everyone set their clocks and watches by the courthouse clock. This charming building was enhanced by a well-manicured lawn, and an elegant fountain with shooting water and colored lights, making it a symphony to watch. To one side of the courthouse was a bandstand. A band concert would be held every Saturday night. Everyone in Dallas enjoyed this weekly event, especially the children.

One afternoon several neighborhood children came to our house to play. One girl started out by saying, "My dad is the most handsome." I finally had to get my two bits in and blurted out, "My dad was in the Navy, and my dad can give the best funerals. Beside that, he is the most handsome." Of course, my friends became curious regarding the part about funerals. "So okay," I said, "we will play funeral." Now mind you, I didn't know any more about funerals than they did, except what I had heard from Mother and Dad. I knew we had to have a body, as Dad would say. I had one of the girls close her eyes and pretend that she was dead. We all gathered flowers and weeds from about the yard. We then carefully placed our bouquets on top of her body and sang Christmas carols.

"The service is over, and it was a beautiful service. Not a dry eye in the house!" I exclaimed. (I had heard this "dry eye" expression from someone. I didn't make it up.) In the meantime, one of the mothers came to take her daughter home. She was horrified to see what was going on. She called my mother right away and with a firm voice announced, "My daughter will never be allowed to play with your girls ever again." Of course, Mother was almost ill over this episode. She didn't realize what we were playing. This was a bitter pill for my mother to swallow, but in time it all blew away. Knowing Aunt Florence, as I do, she probably was responsible for the reconciliation. All of the girls eventually came back, and we were all good friends. Helen and Suzanne Hamilton became especially close friends. Helen and I were close pals, as were Susan and Sylvia. Everyone would be amused with the two of them. What one didn't think up, the other would. They were referred to as "the Two Towheads." The four of us remained close friends through the years.

The change of schools was quite an upset for me, but in a short time that, too, became forgotten. I was pleased with all of my new friends; however, it was Mother who was not content. I remember her saying many times, "I have never seen such a cliquey town." It was a blessing for her that Eunice and Jim Hawke, our best friends who lived on a farm near Dallas, frequently visited. Their visits were especially beneficial for Mother. We loved it, too, when Dad would take us out to their farm. They had a daughter named Mary and a son, Al. Since they were close to our ages, it was more fun than ever. They were the nicest, best-hearted family I have ever known. And what a spectacular farm they had. But it was like Dad said: "Any farm would be terrific with Jim and Eunice

11

Chapter Four

It wasn't more than a year later when Mother began to show signs of illness. She was pale, always tired, and losing weight. She seemed to have a constant cold. It was not a cold, however, it was the T.B. virus. Needless to say, my father was devastated, as was the rest of the family. Mother was sent to the T.B. sanitarium in Salem, which broke our hearts. I will never forget the day when we had to have the inside of our house fumigated, including our clothes. From then on our father watched us like a hawk. He was overly protective regarding our health. Every afternoon we had to have at least a full hour's nap. We ate oranges as though they were going out of style. We drank not just one quart of milk a day, but two.

Then there was the cod liver oil and boring sunbaths. It was a difficult time for two very active girls. It was so embarrassing to have our house fumigated. And how very deplorable it was when we visited Mother for the first time. We were not allowed to touch her, let alone kiss or hug. It was an unforgettable experience. How very terrible it must have been for her. A dark cloud seemed to be hovering over our family.

I became a very lonely girl, but I was fortunate to have my grandmother close. I would spend hours with her. She taught me to sew and make quilts for my doll beds while telling me tales about going over the Oregon Trail. How she laughed when she described how their cream churned into butter from being bumped and sloshed from the hard knocks the wagons had to endure. I was totally fascinated with her storytelling. And how I loved it when she told tales about Mother. "She was the baby of the family and naturally she was spoiled. Her brothers and sisters would grant her every little wish. If she didn't get her way, off she would go on her white horse, Trixie, for hours," Grandma said with a chuckle. But I could tell she was worried about her girl.

Grandma had a small rocking chair out on her porch for Snookie, her cat. I wanted to sit in it just one time. No way, it was Snookie's chair! He would hiss and show his claws if I only walked near him and the chair. Even with Snookie's ugly manners, I still had tender admiration for the adorable little chair. *It would suit and fit me just fine*, I thought.

One day I asked Grandma about the chair. She seemed quite surprised that I was that interested. "Oh! You mean this old chair. Well, now, honeybun, this chair came over the Oregon Trail with me." Then she demonstrated as to how the chair would fold up so that it would lay flat on top of their wagon. "My chair was my luxury so that I could sit with the other ladies around the evening fires."

"And then what did you do?" I asked.

"Oh, just visit, and sometimes we all would sing."

I was intrigued with her stories. Sometimes my imagination would run wild during our visits. I would think she must have known Abraham Lincoln since she was old enough to have gone over the Oregon Trail. Grandmother was such a pretty lady, so Abe Lincoln must have taken her to one of those foxy balls. I was so elated with my discovery I not only told my friends about this great event of Grandma's but I spread the word to perfect strangers. Of course, Dad heard about my story from several different people. We had quite a lengthy discussion concerning Grandma. I explained to Grandma what had happened, and how sorry I was. Several days later the Tillamook relatives came out to Dallas. Aunt Jessie couldn't wait to get at me about the Abe Lincoln story. "How dare you disgrace your grandmother in such a way! You really did hurt her. Abraham Lincoln has been dead for years," she scolded. Well, I guess I learned the hard way. Being old was not to be mentioned.

Aunt Florence later hee-hawed, "Nadine, you reminded me of a tiny Paul Revere, spreading the word!" I had caused quite a stir, and not ever intending to. I depended upon Aunt Florence a great deal, especially for help with homework or for mending a broken doll. She was a great fixer-upper. I loved her, as everyone did.

My father attempted to hire several different housekeepers for our home, but none of them lasted long. I could not tolerate anyone using my mother's things, especially from the kitchen. I must have made them miserable. One day I saw Mrs. Hardy lick a mixing spoon and then put it back into the batter. She was gone the next day. Finally, Dad found a young, pretty housekeeper. Her name was Ruth Evans. We got along famously. She continued to work for us five days a week. She was almost like part of the family. I am positive that she used child psychology, but even she could not push my loneliness aside for Mother. Our fun times and our precious music went away with Mother. It was almost like a summer breeze leaving and the chill of winter arriving.

I have always been grateful for my God-given gift of imagination, even though it has given me trouble when used unwisely. I began drawing and creating my own comic strips. In a way, I was originating my own little world, which was a happy one. It was fun, and entertaining for Dad as well. He could keep me supplied with rolls of grocery paper for my drawing. I would have so much enjoyment reading my comics to my little sister. And what a pleasure for my father, sharing them with Mother.

My father had his hands full with a new business to think about, a wife who was seriously ill, and two girls who required a great deal of attention, so it was marvelous for my dad and uncle to have Paul Bollman come into the business. Paul was a gem of a young man and as time rolled by, I began to think of him as a brother. Aunt Florence said so many times, "Paul is just like part of the family," so having him was wonderful, especially for Dad at this time.

The Barnum and Bailey Circus had come to Salem and just hearing about this thrilling event made my heart fill with excitement. I didn't dream that Sylvia and I would have even a tiny chance of going, so when Dad announced that Uncle Chet and Aunt Florence wished to take Sylvia and me to the circus, I became overly exhilarated with this great news. It was such a thrill for both of us. This was our first circus! Also, it was our first experience being in a huge crowd of people. Aunt Florence took Sylvia's hand and Uncle Chet tightly held my hand. "Step along now before you get stepped on," he would say. I don't really know which part of the circus I enjoyed most. It must have been the girls performing high up on the trapeze. I am sure Aunt Florence and Uncle Chet were having a marvelous time as well, as they were buying us everything that they could get their hands on. I had the feeling when we arrived back home there was a touch of sadness from both of them. When we left them we had a toy monkey on a stick, our first cotton candy, and stars in our eyes that lasted for days. We spent the next day performing on the school equipment, pretending we, too, were glamorous circus stars. We were more like two monkeys swinging on the rings and bars.

Then came that awful day when we decided to make caves in amongst the school's furnace wood which was stacked at least eight feet high, and each piece was five feet wide or more. We would pull out pieces of wood and then crawl into our cave. It not once occurred to us that the huge pieces of wood might roll, which they did! This frightening thing happened with Sylvia and one boy still in their cave. The rumble of the wood and our screams for help brought many neighbors to the rescue while I ran as fast as I could for Dad. When he saw Sylvia pinned in under those massive pieces of wood, he came close to passing out. We all feared she was crushed. It was a miracle that she wasn't. The boy had a broken leg and Sylvia was only badly bruised.

Chapter Five

After this horrifying accident the Hawke's invited Sylvia and me to spend two weeks with them out on their farm. I am sure Dad needed a rest from us. Going to the Hawke farm was like a breath of fresh air for Sylvia and me, even though it wasn't all fun and games. I had so much love and respect for Eunice and Jim Hawke. They gave us chores right along with Mary and Al, but this made me feel important and special because we were doing it for them. Jim sounded serious and, yes, threatening when he made a big announcement: "When you girls are ready to leave the farm, you will have to go out to the barn and get weighed. Every pound you gain will cost your dad a dime." In those days a dime was a lot of money and I wondered how Dad would take it. I believed everything Jim said. When he spoke, I paid attention. He was a rugged man with a Charlton Heston appearance. But when the dinnerbell rang, I ate as much or more than the rest—everything was so good, I didn't worry about the dimes.

The happiest part of the farm as far as I was concerned was Fritz, the powerful male collie. I absolutely adored that dog. He must have been aware of my love for him because I never was out of his sight, except when he was bringing in the cows to the barn. Then, he was not out of *my* sight. I never tired of watching this beautiful animal work. There was a bond between the two of us. Eunice was the first to recognize this. She was amazed to see Fritz sleep under our bedroom window, even though our room was on the second floor. Of course, I always had a special treat for him from the dinner table. (His and my secret.)

There was a delightful wooded area behind the Hawke farm that the four of us and Fritz hiked to every afternoon. We would load up Al's big wagon with all sorts of junk (but very important "junk" to us). Eunice was never too busy to take time to prepare her special lemonade for our fabulous trip.

Before we knew it, the two weeks had come to an end. I was anxious to see Dad but always sad leaving the farm and Fritz. In spite of my mixed emotions, it was exciting to see Dad driving up the narrow, dusty road to the house. Sylvia and I were more than ready to go home, even though we had a joyful time. Now, I almost forgot when Jim, with a twinkle in his eye, said, "You kids better hike to the barn and get on the scales." I got on the scales all right. I stood very still, and held my breath. "You owe me twenty cents, and twenty cents more for Fritz." Dad paid my forty-cent bill and Sylvia's twenty cents. There were chuckles from Jim and Dad, especially over Fritz's "treat" bill. I was thrilled to be going home, but when I looked back and saw Fritz standing alone on the road, I couldn't keep the tears back. I felt he couldn't get along without me. Dad tried to reassure me by explaining that Fritz loved his family and home the same as I loved mine. And besides that, I would be going back to the farm again next year. I always believed my father. After all, he was the smartest man in the world!

We had another very happy surprise before the summer ended. The doctor allowed Mother to come home, as she was very close to being cured. We were so elated with this wonderful news! Sylvia and I were not allowed to be too close to her, but I stood as close as I dared when no one was looking. Being close to her two girls and yet now allowed to touch them was too much, so my Aunt Ada brought Mother a beautiful, chocolate-brown Persian kitten for her to love. This was a wonderful, thoughtful thing for her to do. Mother named the kitten Sugarpie. I wished Aunt Ada had thought that I would have enjoyed a kitten as well. I knew that was a selfish thought.

The doctor said that Mother was not out of the woods yet, and he recommended she should to down to Arizona for just a few months, but she would not go, even though Dad begged. He would have gone and stayed with her. She absolutely refused, and that was that. I felt so sorry for Dad, especially when she announced she was going over to Garibaldi to stay with Ora and Kile, which was the worst thing she could have done in her condition. The damp, cool climate is so harmful for anyone with T.B. But there was one good thing about her being over there— she was happy. She could wander around outside and enjoy Uncle Kile's beautiful vegetable garden and berries and, of course, the flowers, especially the dahlias which flourished in the ocean's cool, misty air.

She loved all of this, including Aunt Ora's marvelous meals. However, she missed Dad and her two girls, so every two weeks we would make the trip over there, which in those days was difficult and tiring. The coast range had nothing but turns, one right after another. I was prone to car sickness and as hard as I tried not to, throwing up was part of the trip. An old American Indian tale, "Men who built the coast highway followed a snake," was why there were so many curves. Of course, I believed everything I was told, but believe me, those curves were treacherous when there were icy conditions. Our little Ford spun out many times during one of our winter trips to Garibaldi. Instead of being frightened, Dad made it all seem like fun. "Here we go. Hang on!" We would squeal and laugh with the excitement! Dad was quite a dad—he could make a game out of most everything. Going back home at night was always sad and quiet. I would look over at Dad and think how brave he was.

I enjoyed school, my friends, and my many visits with Grandma.

Aunt Florence, too, was a big part of my life. But there were times I didn't want to be with real people. Then Ruth and Joyce, my two dolls, gave me the comfort and security I craved. I gave them make believe parties and planned fun things to do. I was their mother and I took care of them as though I was a perfect one. They always looked nice, and they were never spanked. They even had pretend ice cream every day.

I enjoyed going down to the Hamilton's house. One Sunday afternoon I decided to visit Helen, and maybe we could find something fun to do. Her mother was busy frying chicken and Helen was helping by setting the table. I was fascinated with the family—Mrs. Hamilton with her cooking and the two girls helping. Mr. Hamilton and the brother were patiently waiting for dinner. When the five of them finally sat down at the dinner table, Mrs. Hamilton sent me home. I was crushed. I went home and put my doll table out in the middle of the yard and placed Ruth and Joyce in their chairs. We, too, had fried chicken, mashed potatoes, and gravy. I promised them apple pie before they went to bed. I satisfied myself.

Boys terrified me. They delighted in chasing me, untying my sash, or running off with my books, so whenever I would see a boy approaching me on the sidewalk, I would cross the street to avoid him. I asked my dad one day, "Why are boys always pestering and doing mean things all the time?"

He said, "Well, that usually is because they like you."

I could not understand this reasoning, especially when the Fourth of July came. As far as I was concerned, boys became monsters. There is nothing like having firecrackers thrown at your legs. They did it just to hear the girls scream and carry on. I soon discovered that it was our screams they were enjoying, so I decided to grit my teeth and go on about my business. I felt confident that I would be left alone; however, I misjudged one of the boys. Of course, it had to be Jay Eddy with a nasty little garter snake. I knew it would never hurt me, but I was scared anyway. I couldn't stand snakes, so I ran from him and darted into the first store that I came to. Jay and his snake went on down the street. I giggled to myself, knowing that I really tricked him.

It was this grocery store and this day that I will never forget. There was a small group of high school boys talking and laughing together in the rear of the store. They were having a marvelous time. There was one special boy in the group that had me mesmerized. I tried not to stare but I couldn't direct my eyes elsewhere. He was handsome and tall with gorgeous, dark, curly hair. His radiant smile and jovial laugh thrilled me. I stood there for the longest while, staring. And as hard as I tried, my heart would not stop pounding. There was no doubt about it—I was in love! I learned later that his name was Larry Bennett, and I was surprised to find out that his parents were close friends of my relatives and dad. He must be a very nice person, I thought, because his family was so well thought of. I was in a dream world all of my own. And, oh, so much in love! L.B. initials appeared quite often around our house. Every bar of soap had an L.B. carved in the center. My father became disgusted, "Isn't there one bar of soap in this house that is in one piece? What is this L.B. business anyway?"

"This is the person that I am going to marry someday." I couldn't have been more serious.

"You will be in love many times before you marry, believe me. Now, let's keep the soap in one piece." I knew in my heart how I felt; Dad just didn't understand. So I went about my young life believing in my own beliefs.

Sunday morning always meant Sunday school for Sylvia and me. Dallas, it has been said, has a church on most every corner. My folks decided that Presbyterian was the church for us. Mrs. Kurrie was my teacher. I was delighted about this because her daughter and I were great friends at school, so I felt quite comfortable. There was never any dilly-dallying on the way because I was always in a hurry to sing the hymns and sit next to Martha Jean Kurrie. I skipped right along. Sylvia had trouble keeping up. "Well, you two girls are good going to Sunday school," said Mr. Brown. (His name was not really Mr. Brown; however, I don't recall his real name. But I will never forget his face, and his beautiful white hair.) He was raking leaves to burn and I liked stopping for a second just to smell that heavenly fall fragrance of burning fall leaves. "I like going to church because Mrs. Kurrie is my teacher. And we all get to sing."

"Sing for me too," he said.

"I sure will, Mr. Brown." It was special this morning because we had two hymns to sing instead one, so I sang one for me and one for Mr. Brown. Our lesson this Sunday was about Jonah and the whale. I couldn't believe a whale swallowed poor Jonah, and I excitedly said, "Mrs. Kurrie, we learned in school just the other day that a whale's throat is too small to ever swallow a whole man. Don't you remember that, Martha Jean?"

Martha Jean was trying to hush me up while her mother began to reprimand, "Nadine, we never disbelieve what the Bible tells us."

"But Mrs. Kurrie, maybe just once the Bible made a mistake." Mrs. Kurrie became angry with me for disrupting her class and ordered me to go home until I decided to believe what the Bible told us. I left with a lump in my throat. My feelings were hurt and I was frightened that Dad would be furious with me. Then what? I knew well enough "what" it would be—the woodshed! I must have resembled a wilted lily by the time I came back by Mr. Brown's place. He was still raking leaves. "Well, Sunday school must have fallen short today," he said.

"I was sent home, Mr. Brown, and I'm scared Dad will really be mad at me." Mr. Brown persuaded me to tell him what had happened, so I told him the sad story.

With an undertone of amusement he said, "Now, Nadine, the Bible is always right, but we sometimes interpret some of its stories differently. I think Jonah had so many problems and so little faith in God that he was swallowed up by his own weaknesses. His troubles became the whale."

"Do you really think so, Mr. Brown?"

"Well, a whale's throat is too small to swallow a man, isn't it?" he said.

I was enthralled with his explanation. "You sure make good sense, Mr. Brown." And with that I walked as fast as I could back to the church and waited for Mrs. Kurrie to come out to the front steps. I greeted her by saying, "Mrs. Kurrie, I am sorry that I upset you, and I will never do it again because I sure do believe in the Bible." Mrs. Kurrie forgave me, and Martha Jean was still my good friend. Sylvia and I walked our way back home, but not without a happy wave for Mr. Brown. As I waved to him I said, "It is too bad the tree must lose its leaves. They could keep the tree warm."

Summer was an especially fun time for me in Dallas, mainly because of the city park which was so ideal for kids. The swimming pool was the big attraction. From a distance it reminded me of a noisy beehive, but instead of bees came the clear sounds of explosive, happy laughter from children. Loving the water as I did, and sharing this emotion with my friends, I couldn't involve myself fast enough! Who knows, I could have been the loudest squealer in the pool! I was an excellent swimmer for my age, but Dad insisted that I take lessons just the same. "You can't know enough about the water," he would say. In the aftermath of the lessons, a race was scheduled about which we all were excited. Each girl swimmer would have a lifeguard swim beside her for safety. I thought that this was a silly idea until I saw that Larry was one of the lifeguards. The swimming instructor had me placed with one of the other guards, only I wiggled myself around so that I was standing with Larry. The instructor soon escorted me back to my original guard. I must have resembled a mouse the way I shilly-shallied back and forth to Larry's side. The next thing I knew the instructor had me by the arm and with firm, angry steps placed me with my original guard. I was so heartbroken that I couldn't begin to swim, let alone win the race, which everyone expected me to do. Dad couldn't believe it, so I was somewhat humiliated. It took several days to regain my self-composure.

Sylvia and I did need more parental attention and discipline. I was recovering from a broken wrist purely because I had disobeyed and Sylvia was forever getting into trouble. I will never forget the day when she and Dad went to every store in Dallas to pay for all of the candy she

had taken. I thought it was good that we didn't live in a large city because it would have taken weeks to repay the store owners. It was difficult for Dad with all of his responsibilities and serious concerns, so I
knew Mother and Dad were contemplating some sort of a change regarding us. Dad had been persuaded to send Sylvia and me to live with Aunt
Ada and Uncle Frank in Tillamook. We would be closer to Mother, and
we needed someone like Aunt Ada to care for us. This would relieve Dad
a great deal, but how I disliked leaving my friends. And the thought of
missing Dad and Grandma made me feel alone and ill. But then the very
thought of being closer to Mother was a delightful outpouring of love, so
we moved in spite of all the negative feelings.

Chapter Six

There was homesickness at first, but Aunt Ada's gourmet cooking and her exquisite talent for dressmaking became a joyful experience for me, since I adored pretty clothes. We were getting along quite well, and yes, I was even enjoying Uncle Frank. He relished teaching us the Tillamook slogan: "Trees, Cheese, and Ocean Breeze." And was he ever right! He had many funny and historical stories to tell. Both Aunt Ada and Uncle Frank were moviegoers, so this was a real thrill for us. We never missed a new change of films that came to town. Once a week we would drive over to Garibaldi to visit Mother, which was a happy time for all of us. She was so pleased to see us dressed in pretty, fresh dresses. I can still see what seemed like a picture of Mother as she stood with Sugarpie in her arms, explaining to us why the butterflies love the flowering shrub called the "Butterfly Shrub." How her eyes sparkled as we quietly watched hummingbirds creating their marvelous hum as they darted in and around the colorful fuchsias. *Life is so gorgeous*, I thought. And knowing we shouldn't do it, Mother and I would sneak a hug. Aunt Ora would pretend that she didn't see.

Aunt Jessie and Uncle Roy lived only a few blocks away from Aunt Ada's place, so we spent enjoyable times with them, especially with Uncle Roy. I was very fond of him, probably because he didn't expect too much from us as long as we didn't disturb his deep concentration while playing solitaire. He would sit cross-legged in the middle of the living room floor for hours. Not a word was spoken unless Sylvia or I would break the silence. Ellna and Willis never seemed to be around because they were several years older and had different interests.

We were so intrigued with Uncle Roy's yard, mainly because of their beautiful fish pond and banty chickens. They were such busy little chickens, keeping bugs off of Aunt Jessie's gorgeous flowers. It was fun watching them, especially the little, bright-feathered, cocky rooster. One afternoon, when we stopped by their house, we became concerned to see Aunt Jessie very frustrated and searching for their banty chickens, so we began looking for them with her, but to no avail. "Well," she said with a sigh, "I guess I'll have to call the police. Someone must have stolen them."

As she was about to go into the house, her neighbor called to her, "Jessie, did you know Roy is uptown with the banties? He has caused quite a stir!" She was laughing so hard we could hardly understand her.

"Everyone uptown is in hysterics!" Aunt Jessie was speechless, but Aunt Ada doubled up, laughing along with the neighbor's hee-haws. Aunt Jessie was not laughing.

"Here he comes now, Little Uncle Roy walking merrily in his Romeo slippers down the sidewalk with five banty chickens behind him."

"What in the hell do you think you're doing?" Aunt Jessie called out.

He just smiled his usual light-hearted but devilish grin, and not a word was spoken. We learned later from several onlookers that Roy was unaware the chickens had followed him. "Well, I'll be damned," he said when he discovered the chickens. So back home he went with the banties close to the heels of his Romeo slippers. No harm was done.

Adjusting to a new school was especially hard because, of course, we didn't know any of the kids. Aunt Ada was not at all eager to acquaint herself with children. I don't think she knew how. And heaven forbid if her beautiful lawn and flowers would be harmed. We never played in her yard. So it is like they say, First I must become a friend to have a friend. It was exceptional to ever have friends come to our house. This was something we were not used to. I was so excited one day after school when a girlfriend and her brother came over with their bicycles. They were planning to teach me how to ride their bikes. I was sure that it would be all right, as long as we stayed off the lawn. We were having such a good time. The girl's brother was keeping the bicycle steady while I got on and then I had a short, wobbly ride. As I looked up, I noticed Uncle Frank standing in front of the sunroom window watching. It made me very uncomfortable, so we didn't stay out any longer. When we came in Uncle Frank immediately asked. "Who was that boy?" It was quite obvious that he didn't want the boy here again, which seemed strange to me but was really nothing to worry about either, so we went on about our business.

That evening Sylvia and I were having a marvelous time playing on the floor in front of the fireplace. It was close to dinner time. It was cozy and a very enjoyable way to make time go faster. Uncle Frank interrupted me, as he wanted me to look at a funny cartoon with him. He insisted that I sit on his lap while reading to me. I didn't want to but he insisted. He held the paper over me and before I knew what was happening, his hand was between my legs. I started to wiggle myself down, but his other arm held me too tight. He continued to read out loud while his other hand wandered over my body. *He has no business doing this*, I thought. My heart filled with hate for this man. I felt frightened and so alone as my body was being invaded. I didn't know what to do. After all, he was my uncle. I wanted to cry out, but I couldn't. This sexual behavior continued and my fear and disgust grew toward him. I had no one to go to or I *thought* that I didn't have anyone.

School was a blessing for me even though I didn't do well. I would much rather stare out of my classroom window and pretend rather than listen to the teacher. I would imagine that I was on the Hawke farm. I could almost feel the warm, soft, powdery dust on my bare feet as we walked down the narrow road to the woods. I could hear Fritz bark excitedly as we went about our adventure. My mind made all of my thoughts real, and my heart so happy. Nowadays, we could call this "meditation," I am certain. If I wasn't imagining Fritz on the farm, I would think about the Dallas swimming pool. I loved that fresh, cool water. All of this was grand until report cards came out! Aunt Ada was quite concerned about my bad grades, so she had to tell my father. He was most angry with me. "You look smart. Why in Hell aren't you?" he shouted at me. I was crushed by his words. I not only had a dirty body, but now I was also dumb. I tried harder in school but I found that I was so far behind the other kids that it really didn't matter. My teacher referred to me as a dreamer. She didn't know that I was in a beautiful land of pretend.

"Nadine," Aunt Ada called to me. "My lodge is having quite a lovely program and they want ten- and eleven-year-olds to try out for the minuet, which is part of the program." Oh! I was so thrilled. So I tried out, and was chosen. I liked it, the slow, graceful, toe-pointing dance, and with a boy partner. There were several couples and we practiced hard for a month before the program. Aunt Ada made a gorgeous, long, peach-colored dress for me. It had rows of ruffles around the bottom. She curled my hair with a hot curling iron. I felt so pretty that night, and so very excited. I was expressing my love of music for the very first time through a minuet dance. I remember having a little stage fright, but as soon as the music began my heart turned to my new love affair—the minuet. It was a wonderful evening for me. My fears about my uncle were put aside by the joy I felt.

We still visited Mother once a week. And this week she seemed overjoyed, hearing about the minuet. Aunt Ada brought the pretty dress with us for her to see, which I wished we had not done because Mother cried. Mother was not walking around the yard and garden as much as usual. I feared she was not getting well. My preference was to stay inside with her rather than venture outside. Their house and garden was at the foot of a steep forest-covered mountain. We delighted in climbing the trees and allowing our imaginations to run wild, but not this day. I could tell Aunt Ada was disturbed as we drove back to Tillamook.

School was becoming somewhat easier and happier because of more new friends, which was most important in my young life because of my worries and fears. In other words, school was becoming a release for me. I began attending school with great anticipation.

There would be many afternoons that Sylvia and I would go to Uncle Roy's after school, which always pleased me because they were different. Sometimes we would sit in absolute silence while he played solitaire. They had a closet in their entry hall in which a light would turn on when the door was opened. We would amuse ourselves by opening and shutting the door to watch the light. In those days that was something quite elegant.

How wonderful for us when the Good Humor man would drive his wagon down our street, wonderful because Uncle Roy never failed to have a dime for us. This particular wagon was decorated to resemble a bright-colored chicken and the ice cream cones were called "drumsticks." The cones were filled with vanilla ice cream and then dipped into chocolate and chopped nuts. They were delicious, all right. I often think and chuckle to myself about how horrified my mother and father would have been if they could have seen Sylvia and me sitting on the street curb with Uncle Roy while he spit tobacco out into the street. Of course he was somewhat tipsy, which we didn't understand. We were with Uncle Roy and that is all that mattered. Aunt Jessie and Ada were always busy with social affairs. That was why Sylvia and I had many afternoons with Uncle Roy. I am happy for those dear memories.

Since Tillamook was close to the Pacific Ocean, we experienced many bad southwestern storms. It was a very scary ordeal for Sylvia and me at first. It always seemed to come in the middle of the night. Sylvia would always cry and she was great with the shakes. I knew what Dad would do, and that would be to make up stories, so I invented a whopper about a huge man atop a mountain called Thunder. He was very angry so he would chop down trees and roll them down into the valley below. The next morning Sylvia couldn't wait to go outside and see all of the trees. I got past that tale by telling her a fireman cleaned them all up right after they rolled down the mountain. Sylvia got over her shakes and that was the main thing.

One afternoon my father surprised us by driving up to Garibaldi and to Tillamook. I was so overcome with joy that I must have displayed quite a brilliant spectacle until I became aware that Larry was with him. Then I became quite suddenly shy and lost for words. I was truly thunderstruck. They didn't stay long, as I am sure my father was on a business trip, but believe me, I was in another world all my own for days. I was so in love with this young man and wished that I could all of a sudden grow up and he would notice me.

As soon as school was out for the summer, Dad promised to take us back to Dallas for a few weeks. I could hardly wait, just to get away from Uncle Frank. It gave me such a sense of well-being to know that I would feel safe once again. It was just a few days before we were to go home that Uncle Frank and Aunt Ada went out to a lodge function. Sylvia and I were home alone having a grand time up in our room. We were all ready for bed, talking about nothing but going home. It was a bright moonlit night. Our room was filled with its glow and it was because of the excitement of going home and the brightness of the moon that made it difficult to go to sleep. We were just about to drop off to sleep when I was startled to hear our bedroom door open. It was Uncle Frank standing in our room. He came over to my bed, pulled the covers off of me, opened up my pajamas, and stood there looking at my naked body. I was terrified. He stood there for a long time. He didn't touch me, but it was what he said: "You are almost ready for me and we will go *away.*" I was overwhelmed with fear and I became so nauseous I had to vomit.

Sylvia heard all of this and it frightened her. She said, "Nadine, you must tell Dad." I knew that I must go to him, but I was so afraid he wouldn't believe me I decided to tell Aunt Ada first. If I got any sleep that night, it was very little. I was trying to think how I would tell Aunt Ada. What would I say? I knew nothing about these matters. All I knew was that this was happening to me and I knew it was wrong.

The next morning, before school, I approached my Aunt Ada and I said to her, "Aunt Ada, I have to tell you Uncle Frank puts his hands inside of my underwear. And he does this almost every time we are alone. I know that he shouldn't do that." I was one stunned girl when all she had to say was, "Don't tell your dad. He won't let you stay here. Now, you had better hurry on and go to school before you are late." I couldn't believe that she didn't care. There I was, just eleven years old with a huge adult problem and no one to go to. I was too embarrassed to tell Dad and what would I do if he didn't believe me? It was a miracle, I do believe, when out of the blue, I remembered back to that Sunday morning, when Mr. Brown explained to me his interpretation of Jonah and the whale. It was like a lightbulb had lit in my brain and the pounding suddenly left my heart. Quite unexpectedly, I was given the courage to tell Dad about Uncle Frank without embarrassment. I knew he would believe me. I thought to myself, *The old whale almost got me.*

The next day, Father arrived earlier than expected to take his two very elated girls home. If the truth was known, he was every bit as exhilarated as we were. What a happy, fun trip it was for the three of us, even better than Christmas. That night, after dinner, I decided not to delay any longer discussing with Dad the horrible ordeal with Uncle Frank. I told him the entire story, and also the response that Aunt Ada gave. My courageous, fun-loving father turned absolutely ashen and his strong big hands trembled. I cried as I said, "I'm sorry, Dad."

"You were right to tell me. We will go back to Tillamook in the morning and get the rest of your things. Your Aunt Ada was right. I won't let you girls stay another day over there."

The trip back to Tillamook was not a happy one. Instead, we were quiet with long sullen faces. I was grateful though that Dad had called Aunt Ada the night before so she had all our things packed and ready. Dad talked to Uncle Frank before we left. I had never seen a grown man cry before this day. He sobbed with his hands over his face. I couldn't help myself by having feelings of sorrow for him.

That same day the three of us drove on over to Garibaldi. We had to tell our mother what had happened. She knew something was very wrong when we arrived. Naturally, Sylvia and I were directed to stay outside while Dad dreadfully attempted to explain why we girls had to move back home. I will never know if Mother truly believed the shameful happening, as it never again was mentioned by either parent. In other words, it was swept under the rug as if it had never happened. I do know my parents were both devastated, as they had a right to be. Mother was never the same again; her lovely thoughts were clouded with heartache. And even though Dad had always been strict, he became more so, as well as temperamental. "Well, it is over. Now we must start new again," he said, and that is exactly what we did, with many emotional changes and with a great deal of firmness.

Chapter Seven

It was a good thing we both loved to swim because we spent the majority of our summer swimming. "Good for the lungs, especially *your* lungs, Nadine," I heard over and over again. Dad would come down to the swimming pool to check on us, and if I wasn't in the water he would become agitated and order me to get back into the water. Naturally, this was embarrassing to me in front of my friends. I would never disobey my father deliberately. I loved him too much.

My dad and the doctor came to a conclusion that I should learn to play the saxophone. This would be wonderful therapy for my lungs. I was not pleased with this new development. I became more than just a little disgruntled. It was such a big, heavy horn. Why couldn't it be a more feminine instrument like a clarinet or a flute? "You must play something that takes a great deal more lung power," I was told. So I learned to play my dad's sax with protest. The position of the saxophone keys are almost identical to the piano keyboard, so that part was fairly easy for me. But many times I felt as though the back of neck would bleed from the weight of the horn and rubbing of the strap. In spite of all the misery, I did manage to not only blow the horn but also to play a few pieces of music. My father was overjoyed while the neighborhood went crazy. No one was pleased but my dad.

The summer went fast for me with all of the swimming and the hours spent practicing the saxophone. Of course, the highlight of the summer was the annual visit with the Hawkes. It truly was marvelous being with the four of them. And Fritz, with his exuberant greeting, was an enormous thrill for me. *Who loves whom the most?* I wondered. Our visit was as much fun and delightful as ever. It was a perfect way to end the summer.

I was a typical eleven-year-old, so excited to be going back to school and to be with friends whom I had not seen since my return home from Tillamook. My first day was extra special. My second day of school was indeed a catastrophe. My dad, unbeknownst to me, had persuaded the school band instructor to allow me to be a member of the band. I couldn't believe what he had done. I was paralyzed with disbelief. The members were all several years older than me and, most important, they were experienced and confident. I was filled with fear and so very embarrassed. I couldn't go to school so I developed a fake stomachache which Dad became aware of almost immediately. He severely punished me, not by the usual spanking, but by beating me with a stick of wood. He had lost complete control of his temper. I remember my screams, "Please stop, I'm sorry!"

I walked to school the next day not only carrying my books, but also the heavy saxophone case. I attended my first band practice shy and fearful. I could not force even a coy smile when the instructor introduced me to the band members. It was wonderful how they helped and encouraged me. I was not alone anymore and my confidence began to grow. I practiced long and hard every night and, needless to say, Dad was enthused. So enthused, that every time I would learn a new piece of music or accomplish something that was difficult, I would be rewarded. My first was my first permanent wave and when I learned to play *Good Night, Sweetheart*, that was worth my first pair of silk stockings. Mother was more than frustrated with his bribing. "She's learning, Esther. Isn't that the main thing?" he would say. Mother could have cared less whether I played the saxophone or not. She hated my hair. It hurt her a great deal when her girls looked shabby and unkempt. I am sure I resembled someone who had just had an electric shock. As I look back on this I think, *Poor Mother, so helpless, wanting to care and do for her two girls*.

Home became a busy but not a happy place. I would take my homework next door to Aunt Florence for help. I did not always need it but I dearly loved sitting next to her on the porch. I know she loved having me there because she insisted that she read at least one story from her collection of Bible stories especially written for children. They were beautiful stories and the books were also exquisite—blue leather etched in gold with gold binding. They even had their own very small mahogany bookcase. I felt so special as she read to me. If I didn't go to her in the evenings, she would call to me to come on over. I often wondered if she purchased those children's books just for me. I like to think so.

Dad didn't laugh much anymore, he was not at all like he used to be. I wondered many times if he was sick or was it just worry about Mother. Maybe Sylvia and I were just too much trouble. For every mistake or minor mishap, we were severely punished. Now the old jokes about the woodshed were no laughing matter at our house. We would be beaten and every blow would bring a scream. I thought I would die listening to my sister. I would beg him to take me to the shed first so that I wouldn't have to hear her screams.

Bless the old living room rocker. It provided comfort against our physical pain and shattered egos. We would huddle close together and rock as hard and as fast as we could while gulping back the sobs. Dad would be sitting in front of the kitchen table with his head cradled between his arms, crying like a child. I wondered, *Why do you do this, Dad, when it hurts you so much?* I could never understand.

We could always depend on him to ease his conscience by treating us to the movie theater. Suddenly, everything was all right for Sylvia and me at the time. In those days we had gorgeous musicals to watch. I loved the music and especially the dancing. My imagination led me into the movie screen. I became the leading lady. I was the one wearing the lavish costumes and it was my legs and feet doing those fantastic and sometimes wild dances. I would be in a dream world after one of these movies. The old porch became my stage and I would dance and dance. One day I wondered that maybe if I jumped from the porch banister and kept my feet moving at the same time, I might fly like a bird. Unknown to me, Aunt Florence was my audience from her window and it was she who persuaded Dad to give me dance lessons. I begged for ballet, but, no, it had to be tap or nothing at all. So tap it was. I enjoyed it, even if it wasn't ballet. With schoolwork, the saxophone, and now tap dancing, I was a busy girl.

My first band concert was a real big deal for me. It was so exciting. I had to sit at the end of the row on stage, otherwise I would have never been seen. I did have trouble keeping my feet flat on the floor because my legs wouldn't stretch any longer. I managed to keep up with the rest of the band, except now and then my reed would squeal like a terrified pig. I would be so embarrassed, especially when Mike Peters, my friend, shouted from the audience, "That's the Thomas girl!" I was afraid of what Dad would say, as he could not tolerate mistakes, but he never mentioned the squeals, so he must have been proud. He didn't say, or maybe he just couldn't.

We were making more frequent visits to Garibaldi because Mother was not getting well. If anything, she was getting worse, though I would never admit it to myself. I felt that she was just unhappy or homesick, so I did everything I could think of to make her laugh or just smile. Our trips over and back were filled with sadness. I never lacked that little spark of hope that just maybe today would be different, Mother won't be coughing today. She might even be sitting up in bed looking pretty with pink cheeks. Mother had beautiful skin and when she felt happy she would always have that lovely pink glow. That was what I prayed to see.

It is amazing how life does go on in spite of dark clouds of worry. There was school every morning, my saxophone, and, oh yes, the dance lessons. Sometimes the days went super well and then there were those when, naturally, nothing went right.

It is strange how the holidays, including Christmas, are a complete blank for me during Mother's illness, except for one Thanksgiving at Aunt Florence's lovely home. Her dinners were always elegant and delicious. What really stuck in my mind was the hot and heavy argument over politics. I was fascinated as their tempers flared. I am sure that I resembled someone who was watching a Ping-Pong match, and I became excited wondering who was going to win. Uncle Chet stood by himself defending the Republicans. My dad and others were for the Democrats. Uncle Roy, a Republican, didn't even say boo. Uncle Roy just sat there with a tickled grin on his face. The argument ended with Uncle Chet standing up from the table and making a very firm statement. "You'll see that in six months I was right!" I did hear many times, "Well, Chet was right," so I decided then and there to save a lot of time. I went along with Uncle Chet's ideas.

This eleventh year of my life was a sad time for me. I painfully could see Mother fading away from us, slowly but surely. Why wouldn't God answer my faithful prayers? Why was Dad becoming more hostile towards me than ever before? I could not understand. The beatings were more frequent regardless of my well-thought efforts. I tried so very hard to please. It was a blessing for me to have my grandmother near. I spent as much time with her as I dared. They were blissful visits filled with the pleasure of just being together. Her pretty, pink candy dish would be filled with peppermints. And if the drugstore had pink peppermints, that is what we would have because the pink ones tasted the best. She loved me, and I knew it!

It was good that I began enjoying school and the band was becoming loads of fun as well as challenging. Mrs. Cerny was a favorite teacher of mine. I adored her. One day after school she said to me, "My heavens, Nadine. How on earth can you carry that heavy horn home every day?"

"Oh, I walk, then I stop and rest, then I go a little farther and rest some more."

"Well," she said, "I am sure Mike would carry your saxophone home for you. How about it, Mike?" she asked him. He was more than pleased and I thought this was great! We were good school friends. I still remember how he showed off. He was strong and he made sure I noticed. We both were having fun laughing and clowning around, as all kids do at that age, until we were almost past the mortuary. My dad saw us and he became furious. He left the building in a rage. He grabbed the saxophone case from Mike and pulled me home by my arm. I was brutally beaten. Eating dinner that evening was impossible and sleeping on my bruised back was too painful. Mike was one-half Native American. "Don't you ever bring that half-breed home again," Dad kept repeating. Mrs. Cerny must have learned about this awful scene because never again did she volunteer help for me from Mike or anyone else.

There were no words of praise from my father. My grades were never good enough. He was convinced that I could always do better. Nothing that I did seemed to please him. Then came the morning that I couldn't find a thing suitable to wear for school. "I can't go to school today, Dad," I announced.

"I would like to know why," was his reply.

"Because I don't have a thing to wear. Nothing I have fits."

"You have clothes, young lady. Now get dressed," he ordered. So I took a pair of scissors to a dress which was too short, and I cut the skirt off. I wore it as a blouse with my one and only wool skirt. He was stunned and surprised to see what I had done. I went on to school feeling very self-complacent. I, for once, pleased myself with a spark of cleverness. After school that day, Dad and I went shopping with no explanations and no apologies. He behaved as though it was his discovery that new clothes had become essential, and I certainly was not about to dispute him. We both had a marvelous time shopping. I was thrilled and excited by his attention.

Even though I enjoyed school, it was exciting when summer vacation finally arrived. With the very thought of summer, my attention turned entirely to swimming. Swim I did, and I think if I could have gotten away with it, I would have lived down at the park.

This was the summer that Uncle Chet and Aunt Florence went to the Chicago World's Fair. Instead of a homecoming filled with excitement, there was nothing except hushed voices. Occasionally, I would hear an "Oh no" or "How could this be? Florence has always been so healthy. She is never sick." Finally, Dad explained to us that Aunt Florence's right foot would drag and that she had pain in the back of her neck when she tried to lift her right foot. This happened to her while they were sightseeing in Chicago. My heart sank. I felt such fear for my beloved aunt. "I know Chet is worried sick. I only wish I could do something," Dad would say. We all felt so helpless, especially when Uncle Chet was taking her to many different doctors and none of them could help. How could we help when the doctors didn't even know what the problem was?

A dream of pleasure had turned into a nightmare; another dark cloud hovered over our family. This was a confusing, difficult time for me because I began to feel guilty having fun when there was so much trouble at home. Why should I have the right to swim and laugh when Mother was so sick and Aunt Florence couldn't walk? Life seemed so unfair, so I said to Aunt Florence one day, "Aren't you mad at God?"

She was dismayed with me as she said, "Don't ever think or speak of God that way. He is my only hope." I was a humiliated, disgraced eleven-year-old girl because of my own negative thoughts. No one could put me in my place like Aunt Florence because I held her in such high esteem and respected her. She said, as I was leaving, "By the way, Nadine, people do not get mad, only dogs."

It was a short visit but quite advantageous. Jonah and the whale came back to me. This very thought stunned me: The whale almost had me.

So now and then I began to think how fortunate I was to have so many fun-loving girlfriends with kind, gentle parents. Martha Jean and her parents, the Kurrys, were so wonderful to me. Both Mrs. and Mr. Kurry treated me as though I was their other daughter, so I always felt comfortable and content to be with them. They lived on a small farm just outside of Dallas. Mr. Kurry was an insurance man and during his spare time he was a farmer. It would make me feel wanted when I was asked to do a chore. What a thrill it was when Mr. Kurry would bring Jake, the workhorse, from the barn to be harnessed up for a heavy task. Martha Jean and I thought it great sport riding behind Jake and Mr. Kurry. Now, Martha Jean and I would have taken a prize for giggling and this particular day was no exception. Jake must have eaten too much grass or whatever, and every time he made a turn he would loudly expel gas. At first we ignored Jake and pretended not to hear. Oh yes, we were ladies about the entire affair, but not for long. We didn't dare look at one another without going into a fit of snickers. My sides hurt from trying not to laugh. Mr. Kurry was so doubled-up he couldn't speak. I don't know if he was laughing at us or with us. I really was relieved when the ride was over so that we could run for the ice house and allow our agonizing giggles to explode into a rolling laughter. That is exactly what we did while enjoying a bottle of Mrs. Kurry's homemade root beer. When the ice cold root beer hit my stomach, there was a rebellion. I burped, then we both burped and not dainty-like, either, but man-sized. My nose felt as though it was on fire. We were miserable, but silly. I would say we were two normal, happy girls enjoying a summer afternoon on the farm. Mrs. Kurry made powerful root beer, but it wasn't strong enough to cure our foolishness. I loved being at the Kurry's place because they were lively, busy, and so very good-natured. We were always ready for bed when the time arrived, plum tuckered out! But on this night, low and behold, a bat flew into our bedroom! We screamed, piercing Mrs. Kurry's ears. She tore into our room, not knowing what had happened, only to discover a terrified but harmless bat. Clad in her long, white, flannel gown, she scurried madly for a broom. After chasing the scared, frightened bat around for what seemed like hours, she finally sent the poor, terrified critter out through the open window. I awakened the next morning with the covers still over my head.

Chapter Eight

What excitement there was at our house when Dad announced to Sylvia and me that we were going to spend a week in Barview, which was near Garibaldi, so that we could see Mother every day. He had rented a cabin and Ruth agreed to go with us to care for our needs. I was beside myself thinking about seeing Mother every day and the rest of the time we could enjoy the beach and the ocean. There was also a beautiful small lake surrounded by sand hills, low-growing scrubby trees, and bushes. The lake's water was only cold enough to be refreshing. It wasn't just any lake, however. I felt that God created it especially for me. In my own mind it was my lake. The ocean and the beach were over to the left side of the lake's sand hill; so ideal, so perfect for a vacation. There was also a jetty that persons old and young enjoyed exploring and experienced the powerful energy of the surf. It would be a mistake if I did not mention the exciting act of fishing from the jetty's huge, mammoth rocks. In those days the jetty was indeed a popular place. The Coast Guard station at that time was located in Barview, which to me was a beautiful sight with its spotless, pure white buildings and immaculate green lawn. It reminded me of a painting. I was truly enthralled to think I would soon be spending an entire week in Barview, so near to Mother. We were especially grateful to spend time at the coast because this particular August was unusually hot and dry. It was too hot and uncomfortable for most adults, but for me it was a great excuse to spend more time in the lake.

We left early the next morning for the coast and I must admit the anticipation of seeing Mother and the eagerness for Barview made the drive seem endless. When we arrived, Aunt Ora and Uncle Kile welcomed us warmly. I was so thrilled to be out of the car and finally inside this friendly home of Aunt Ora's, and now, at last, I could see my darling mother! She appeared so small, weak, and pale, but her eyes were overflowing with joy and love. I virtually could not focus on her physical condition. Before we left Garibaldi for Barview, Mother said to me very confidentially, "Nadine, when I see you tomorrow I want to have a private little talk with you. A 'mother and daughter visit' if you will."

How very special, I thought. I had never had a mother and daughter talk before. How marvelous and important. Now I could say, "I, too, had a mother and daughter talk." Now I could be like the other girls.

"Hello, Barview. Hello, Lake!" I went wild. I couldn't get into my suit fast enough! It was wonderful, my lake! I had her all to myself and it was every bit as marvelous as I had imagined. Such fun we had on the beach, and the special walks out on the jetty with Dad were just scary enough to become exciting! Of course, my favorite time was spent in the lake. We almost always had the lake to ourselves because strangers didn't have a clue there was a hidden lake between the sand hills.

I made sure that I would have my mother all to myself for this very important mother and daughter talk. Mother was so cute in the manner she used to hustle the family from her room. I sat beside her as she affectionately placed her hand on my leg. Having her to myself for this short time has been a treasured memory through my years. She became quite serious as the very important talk began. The talk was as important to her as for me. She, very gently and with loving care, explained the menstrual cycle to me. I didn't say a word about the older, smug girls who already had alerted me, leaving me confused and apprehensible. So, being human, my thoughts became negative and fearful.

There were many questions for my mother. "It is only when we don't understand something that we become fearful," she said. By the time our conversation was over I began to understand that it all was very normal and positive. Mother went on to tell me that when my time came not to hesitate to go to my dad. I had experienced my one and only "mother and daughter talk."

Our third wonderful day was interrupted by a strong smell of smoke and a dark, gray sky. Dad had just heard rumors that east of Tillamook a forest fire was turning ugly, so he decided that we should drive over to Tillamook to find out for ourselves just how serious this was. The closer we came to Tillamook, the darker it became. I sensed the concern Dad was feeling and I became uneasy. It seemed to be happening with so much fury. The smoke came in such haste. All of sudden there was smoke everywhere. Dad was searching for Uncle Roy, as he would have knowledge regarding the fire. We found him uptown. It was amazing that we recognized him. He was wearing sunglasses and a handkerchief covered his nose and mouth. He was protecting his eyes, nose, and mouth from the smoke and cinders. My first reaction was that Uncle Roy looked like a bandit, but I knew better than to say it. Breathing the smoke was indeed miserable.

Yes, Uncle Roy had all of the news and we learned from him how very serious the fire was. It was worse than anyone dreamed, and spreading in spite of the truckloads of firefighting men. The C.C.C. (Civilian Conservation Corps), logging crews, and men from the sawmills were struggling with the rapid flames. The dry, hot wind and the extremely low humidity was the fiendish enemy. We also learned that we were not to travel back into the valley because of the fire dangers. Not until we had the okay from the fire officials could we go home. The thought of being almost completely surrounded by fire gave me a chilling, eerie sensation. We drove back to Garibaldi, and later to Barview and prepared ourselves for a longer stay. By late afternoon the smoke in Garibaldi was much worse, which made it extremely difficult for Mother to breath, so Uncle Kile and Dad arranged sprinklers around the house especially close to Mother's room, which made breathing easier for her. We all were worried about Mother, especially Dad.

By evening the sky was completely red and the reflection made everything turn into a hazy shade of red. Everything was red, including us. We were in a strange, strange world. Even the ocean had become a bright red. A swim in the lake was like a swim in watercolor paint. The next morning we not only found a rosy-colored lake but it was also black with cinders. Our beautiful white sand, too, was covered with ashes and cinders. There was not a bird in sight. Not even a gull.

It was amusing to watch Uncle Kile fuss over his chickens. No way would they leave their cozy, comfortable henhouse and go out into this dark, spooky world. Of course, since they thought it was night, all of Uncle Kile's coaxing wouldn't budge them. The dairymen had the same problem with their cows. They had no intention of leaving their barn. It was horrible hearing so many frightening experiences of people who narrowly escaped with their lives. We heard about families leaving their campsites by riding over burning railroad trestles. It was said that the fire was like a hurricane and its force was inconceivable. Everyone was in awe of the forty-mile-wide cloud of smoke that mushroomed up into the sky. It surely explained our darkness. My miserable upset was with the wild animals and their dangers. I made myself ill with worry and concerns for them. If only we could do something! Dad was becoming quite agitated with me. "Well, there is nothing that you can do about it. The only time to worry is when you can do something about it. Looks like the cat might be hungry." I glanced down at Sugarpie. She was under Aunt Ora's feet pestering for something to eat. Dad made his point, all right. But as hard as I tried I felt as much pain as ever for the wild animals. However, I did learn a worthwhile lesson just the same. I turned my worry into willingness to love and help those near to me. Sugarpie more than responded to my attentions. Uncle Kile appreciated my concerns and help with his chickens. Well, I think he appreciated it, but he probably was just being nice, as he was such a kind, patient man.

It wasn't until the end of August before we could go home. However, the fire continued to burn through September. The Tillamook Burn destroyed what many called an empire of fine old timber. It was an unbelievable nightmare, even to this day!

It was exciting to be back home, but how much happier we all would have been if Mother and Sugarpie were here with us, and I wondered about our Aunt Florence. Could she be better? Wouldn't it be wonderful if she could walk without her cane? I am sure my face expressed sadness when I saw her because she said, "No, my dear, if anything I am worse. But that doesn't mean someday that I won't be well." Aunt Florence was always cheerful and positive. "You girls and your dad surely will be going down to the big picnic tonight?" she questioned. Oh my gosh! With all of the excitement of being home I almost forgot about the big picnic which was held down at the city park. So hurry, hurry! First, I had to find Sylvia, which was never easy. She and Suzanne were always somewhere other than home. I found her in time to change into proper attire. As I was changing my clothes, I discovered a tiny drop of blood and I was terrified. What could I do? Mother said to tell Dad, but he wasn't home. So don't be a cry baby, I told myself. Dad will soon be home. And he was, thank heavens. He called out to us, "You kids better hurry up. It's time to go."

Sylvia was all ready and I was like a bump on a log. I whispered into Dad's ear as to what had happened to me. I was so frightened and wishing Mother was there, but Dad was delighted, smiling from ear to ear. "I'll be darned. Now I have a young woman for a daughter." He gave me a big hug and with it he gave me perfect instructions. I was just fine. And I loved thinking that now Dad and I had our own secret. We wouldn't tell a soul except Mother! I felt so grown up with a precious secret. The three of us went to the park picnic. It was the last big park affair before school with lots of scrumptious food and fun games.

I began my seventh grade that year. I do believe this was the hardest year with so many new challenges and most meaningful subjects. What a relief it was when we could go to gym class. I believed that I would be the first to be in my gym shorts and be out on the gym floor. I loved all of the sports, especially the basketball, probably because I had so much pent-up energy. It was such a glorious feeling to rid myself of overflowing, zealous steam. Between the homework, playing in the band, and tap dancing lessons, I was almost too busy, so I plunged into the seventh grade in an assiduous manner. It was exciting; a little scary; and, yes, exhausting. I never wished or thought about being popular as a young girl because in my own shy way I had many exceptional, loyal friends. They alone made going to school a true pleasure. Therefore, I didn't have any reason to wish or think about popularity.

Before the school bell rang this Monday morning, several of us huddled together discussing artistic abilities and talents, so I became anxious to tell about and display Dad's fantastic drawings. The next day I displayed Dad's cartoon of Mrs. East which, by the way, was my favorite. The girls were so amused and delighted. "Oh, it looks jut like her!" they exclaimed with so much enthusiastic joy. I guarded the drawing with much caution and care. After the girls had seen it. I painstakingly placed it back into my notebook. All of a sudden a girl named Arlene grabbed it away from me and proceeded to tear it into pieces. I was stunned, as were my friends. *Why did she do this?* I wondered as I gathered up the damaged drawing. I was too stunned to cry. I never really recovered from this hurtful happening because I couldn't understand why she did this hateful deed to me. I didn't even know her. I only knew that her name was Arlene and that she had red hair and freckles. I stayed as far away from her as I could. I went about my business, so to speak. I studied hard and my grades were good, but not as favorable as Dad thought they should be, so naturally I was not pleased with my efforts. I did enjoy the band. It was neat to be able to keep up with the other members and not make noticeable mistakes. Tap dancing was okay, but I would have traded my taps any day for a pair of ballet slippers. *That is okay*, I would think. *My day will come*. What an excellent dreamer I was. Whenever I became unhappy, my dreams so often would bring contentedness.

Our gym class was really getting into the game of basketball and I was crazy about it. I was so involved with the competition and skills I couldn't see anything else but the game. Energy? I had enough for two girls. After one of the games my friend Pat said to me in a informative tone, "Nadine, do you know why those older boys always sit over there on the bench?"

"No, why?" I responded.

"Because of your legs," she said.

"Pat, that is dumb. Boys are dumb." I was embarrassed and upset.

"Just the same, they like your legs" Pat said.

"No boy is going to ruin my basketball game, legs are legs." As far as I was concerned, a boy was nothing more than a big bother and a bore. Of course, if Larry had so much as given me a glance, I would have gone into a heavenly dither.

We were making trips more frequent to Garibaldi these days, and I knew it was because Mother was failing. I could see how thin she was becoming and her coughing at times must have been torturous. Even though she was extremely ill, she did appear to enjoy hearing about school and my thrill of playing basketball. During one of our visits she made quite a point of telling me to always follow my talents and "Never think for a minute that you can't. You are given a talent for a reason." At that time her words really didn't sink in, but later in life they surely did.

In the meantime, the citizens of Dallas began planning their big Halloween costume parade. This was one of the most important events of the year. The adults of Dallas would begin displaying their enthusiasm with new ideas and methods. Each year was to be better than the year before. I believe this was the beginning of my becoming such a lover of all seasons. Summer was over, so now it was time for crisp freshness in the air we breathed. There were pumpkins, scary costumes, and apple cider. Even the trees showed off by turning their leaves into rich gold and red shades. Only the fall season can do these beautiful things. My happy thoughts were most eager to be in the midst of all of this joyful fall planning. With it came party hubbub.

I was thrilled to be invited to one of the parties. I was excited to hear about apple-dunking, and what fun it would be to take a bite of a swinging doughnut from a string! I literally tingled with jubilation. I was going to a real, honest to goodness Halloween party after the big parade. It was difficult to keep my excitement simmered down until I broke the news to Dad. I knew how pleased he would be for me. The minutes seemed like hours before he finally came home. I greeted him in such a silly, giddy manner that he had to stop and calm me down. "Now start over again, and make sense this time," he demanded.

So in a dancing mode and with a song in my voice, I said, "I am going to a real Halloween party!" I squealed and whirled with delight. Much to my amazement, he did not seem at all pleased with me.

"When and where is this party to be?" he asked. Then I told him it was to be after the parade and the party would be at Pat's house. "I suppose there will be boys there. Is that right?"

"I really don't know, Dad," I answered. I knew well enough that he thought I wasn't telling the truth, and I hadn't the slightest idea who all was invited,

My heart fell a mile when Dad said, "You can go to the parade but you cannot go to the party."

I was so disappointed and furious that I grabbed my coat and threw it with such force that one of the wooden buttons broke in two. My angry father reached for me in such strong displeasure that I broke away from him and ran. I kept running and running because I knew I was in real trouble. I would rather have died than to have another beating. I finally slowed myself down to a walk and I continued walking until it was dark. I was outside of Dallas, past the lumbermill and over a steep hill of fruit orchards. It had become quite chilly and I was tired. Maybe Dad would be so happy to see me that he would forget the woodshed, I thought. But I kept walking; however, much slower. I was becoming scared. Every crackly sound and shadow was chilling me to the bone. I suddenly turned around and briskly walked back home. There were no "Hellos"; no nothing except a small dinner and a reminder that it was past my bedtime. I learned the next day from Ruth that Dad had called Tony the city policeman. Oh my gosh, I was horrified.

"Your father was ill with worry," she said.

Little did I realize this frightening episode ended our fears of the woodshed. Someone out there was much stronger than the whale!

I was smart enough to never mention the party again, so I gladly satisfied myself with the traditional Halloween parade, which was filled with more gusto than ever before. The colored lights of the unique city fountain danced through the geysered water fountain. I was spellbound by its beauty. The lively sounds of the city band's music poured down the street as we children marched with gleeful hearts and scary costumes. We all received treats from the merchants when the parade was over. And, yes, our protective father was waiting for us at the end of the parade to see us safely home. It was a wonderful Halloween.

Chapter Nine

In spite of our concerns regarding Mother, Dad made sure we didn't sit around home with long, sad faces. We were kept busy. I don't believe the three of us missed one new movie that came to town. These were the days of fabulous, extravagant musicals which dazzled and overwhelmed me. The unique, lively music and dancing kept my young mind and heart full of inspiration, and my imagination went wild.

Dad was making the trips to Garibaldi without Sylvia and me, so I knew Mother must be worse. I did overhear that she was too weak to walk. I prayed harder than ever. "Please make Mother well. Please don't take her away from us." Over and over I would plead with God. But that January fourth a telephone call came informing us that mother was gone. God didn't hear me. My heart became so heavy with sorrow that every part of my body was in pain. It hurt me to look at Dad, knowing and feeling his agony. And poor Grandmother. Her heart must have broken into a million pieces. She had lost another child. The very thought of never seeing Mother, touching, or hearing her again brought an icy, cold circle around me. I began shaking like a wind-blown leaf. My concerned father wrapped heated blankets around me. I must have fallen asleep because the next thing I remember it was morning.

Mother's funeral was my first funeral experience, and I proudly contained my composure until the music selections, *In the Garden* and *I Love You Truly*, were sung. I managed to restrain the painful, swelling lumps in my throat, but my uncontrollable tears escaped and streamed down my face. My inner spirit, being so very sensitive to music, cried inside of me. I huddled as close as I could to Dad without being obnoxious. I wanted him to be my daddy this day, so he was! What was it that closed my eyes? I did not see my mother in her casket, even when all who viewed her exclaimed as to how beautiful and natural she appeared to them. Today, I thank God for closing my eyes so that I remember her as she was—her loving, comforting ways; her music; and that gorgeous, shy smile. Dad said many times, "It was your mother's shy ways that I first fell in love with."

The days after the funeral were difficult. I hated it when well-meaning, motherly women would come up to me with extended arms and smother me with their hugs. "I know how you feel, dear. It is so hard," they would say. How did they know how I felt? They were not me. I squirmed away from them. Genuine compassion and understanding from the heart apparently doesn't always come easy to some people. Children can surely feel the difference.

We forced ourselves to be busy after Mother's funeral and, of course, Sylvia and I went back to school as usual. The first day I felt as though the kids were staring and feeling sorry, which was difficult to accept. But before the week was over, everything was more comfortable. The sadness reminded me of a rubberband snapping back into a more happy place.

I learned at an early age how valuable physical exercise can be for troubled minds. I wore myself to a frazzle on the school's gymnastic bars and rings. Of course, basketball was more important than ever. Yes, I would say that the three of us were doing remarkably well. We watched out for one another and in doing so we became extremely close. I noticed Dad was behaving as though he had his hand caught in the cookie jar. I knew that something was about to happen. And I knew right away what it was when he asked. "Do you remember when I read to you about the air-flow Chryslers and DeSotos?"

"I sure do, Dad. When are you going to get one?" I asked him.

"I shouldn't, what will people say?"

Ignoring his negative attitude, we three strolled over to Smith's garage only to look at and admire those gorgeous new cars. Dad walked around one beautiful powder blue DeSoto, not just once, but more than a hundred times. Then he stood back and said with a smile, "Yeah, I'm going to have that car!" In a few days this heartthrob of a car was his. Never before had I seen my dad radiate such jubilance. He drove me to school the next morning, but he drove in to the back of the school so that we wouldn't be noticed. After I thought about this for awhile I began to understand his feelings. Those were the years of the great Depression.

Our first drive with the new car was out to the Hawke's farm. It was a beautiful clear day, and I just knew it was made special for us. *Dad is as sunny as the sky*, I thought. He was filled to the brim with bubbling enthusiasm and exuberance. Seeing my father like this gave me such joy that I too fell in love with this beautiful blue car. It was like a present from God; so special. The drive was breathtaking in more ways than one. Dad had the speed up to eighty miles an hour on the straight stretches. This speed was something in those days, and I liked it because the thrill of it made me laugh. The Hawkes were surprised and pleased to see us and, as you can imagine, they, too, were thrilled with the car. So gorgeous was this automobile, and so far ahead of its time! They were overwhelmed. As we were getting ready to leave for home, Mrs. Hawke said to us, "You girls take good care of your dad."

Ruth, her soon-to-be husband, and friends from Sheridan were frequent visitors in our home. They hadn't come often while Mother was living but now their visits were quite often. They would arrive after

Sylvia and I were in bed. I tried not to let it bother or annoy me because Dad did need friends and some fun in his life. I knew this, but there was something that disturbed and upset me a great deal, especially when the nights became boisterous with joking and laughing to the point where sleep was almost impossible. Many times we both would be scared, especially Sylvia, and then she would cry. I would invite her to crawl into my bed with me and we would visit. I made up stories which, bless her heart, she believed. In time we both would fall asleep.

I knew well that I must complain to Dad because of his friends' noise. "It is scaring us, Dad, and even Sylvia cries. Neither one of us can go to sleep." Then I asked him, "Who is this Mary? She sure is loud!"

He replied by telling me, "Mary is only a friend. And I am sorry we have been so upsetting for you. It won't happen again." Then he went on to tell me that we were going to Garibaldi that Sunday to bring Sugarpie back home. "How about that?" Dad announced with a sparkle in his eye. How excited we were. I didn't think Sunday would ever arrive. But of course it did, in spite of our impatience. Not once did it occur to me how much courage would be expected to just walk into Aunt Ora's house with Mother not being there. It hit me like a ton of bricks. But I saw how brave Dad was and I knew I dare not show any distress in front of him or Sylvia, so I kept my thoughts only about Sugarpie. There she was, her sweet, fluffy self! Sylvia and I loved her so much. We couldn't express enough affection fast enough. We both were in need of a pet, that was quite obvious. Aunt Ora had her own cat, so she and her cat must have been delighted as well.

Oh all of the fussing Sylvia and I went through on the way home! We both sat in the back of the car with Sugarpie in her box between us. She grumbled and hissed, showing her displeasure constantly. We were sure she would never be the same. She might have been too hot, she may have been carsick. Between the two of us we thought of everything that could have been wrong. Poor Dad must have aged ten years. I don't know which one was more pleased to be home, Sugarpie or Dad. We were elated to see Sugarpie adjust immediately to our surroundings. Of course, she had begun her life here with Mother, we remembered. Sylvia and I coaxed her to sleep on our beds, that is, when we thought Dad wasn't looking. He didn't have to look, he already knew! Sugarpie was happy loving her two girls. Yes, it was a happy day, but a sad one, too. I began to cry for Mother that night and as hard as I tried I couldn't stop. I was afraid that I would waken Sylvia, so I left my bed and went into the living room. I was startled when I saw Dad doubled-up on the couch sobbing his heart out. I went to him, and instinctively my arms went around him and he held me close. Together we cried, as our hearts were breaking together. As I look back at those next few weeks, I realize it was the caring of one another that lifted my spirit above my sorrow. I could not bear the hurt I felt watching my father grieve or even resemble unhappiness, so my thoughts and actions were of him.

The third of February finally arrived. My big birthday, and now I had arrived—I was at last in my teens. Dad surprised us by taking us out to dinner. We always had walked to the restaurant, but this special night Dad drove us there in our gorgeous blue car. I was all atwitter. It was difficult to sit still, let alone taste food. When Dad gave me my first wrist watch, I was out of my mind. Dad was fun again. He even played his sax when we went back home and he also performed by standing on his head so that Sylvia and I could scramble for his loose coins. He also had many magic tricks which absolutely would excite and spellbind us with wonderment.

There never were any dull times in our home. Something always seemed to be happening, and it seemed good. We were becoming a fun family once again even though there were but three of us. "Leave it to Roy," I heard Dad say as he laughed uncontrollably. I was horrified while Dad explained to Ruth as to what was so funny. It seems as though a corpse sat up in his casket during the service. "This funeral was for a very prominent person in Tillamook," Dad was explaining.

"My heavens," Ruth gasped. "What did the congregation do?"

"They went to pieces, of course, and one woman fainted. Roy, well he was in the back of the church when this happened. And I had never before in my life seen Roy hurry, but there is a first time for everything. He no sooner said, 'Jesus Christ,' when he was down front tending to the body. Just that quick!"

One thing about it, Uncle Roy gave Tillamook something to talk about for years to come and not just in Tillamook. The yarn spread over many miles. I hoped Aunt Jessie wasn't angry with Uncle Roy, which was my first reaction. Nothing should go wrong for Uncle Roy, my friend!

We all knew spring was springing in Dallas because Grandma, sure enough, was out snooping and poking in the soil, fussing impatiently and wondering if this or that plant had survived the winter. If she couldn't tell for sure, then she would scatter the soil about until she found her treasure, the adorable crocus. "The first sign of spring," she would say with a cheerful ring of relief in her voice.

Aunt Florence, well, one would never know about her crippled leg by the remarkable way she managed her wicker laundry basket full of freshly washed clothes. She hung each piece of laundry with such perfection. "You never know who might see my washing, so it must look nice. Ah, it already has a sweet aroma," she said with such satisfaction.

Yes, it was spring at home and I loved every bit of it. It also was time to dilly-dally after school, swinging on the rings and bars, just having freedom to dream and time to be silly. Wonderful, that lackadaisical sensation. "I think I'll go over to the other side of the schoolyard and

43

walk along the retaining wall." I thought it might be fun to do, as I had seen other kids doing it. The wall was at least eight feet above the sidewalk. I felt as though I was a circus performer having a marvelous time. As I was coming to the end of the wall I suddenly felt a strong push. I painfully fell down to the rough, paved sidewalk. My books and papers went flying with me. Arlene was looking down at me. I couldn't get up at first, and I am sure this frightened her. I must have been knocked unconscious for a second or so. "I'm sorry, I'm sorry," she kept repeating. "I didn't mean to." I couldn't speak out and I wasn't about to cry, but I did eventually manage to gather up myself, my books, and my pride, and head for home. My legs and arms were bloody and my dress was torn, but I was very fortunate not to have broken bones.

I only had two dresses to my name, so my torn dress was a true catastrophe. How could I ever explain this to Dad when I couldn't explain it to myself? I never did tell him I was pushed from the wall, only that I had *fallen* from the retaining wall. "Well, you sure began spring with a bang, didn't you!" Dad said. It didn't take long for my cuts and bruises to heal, and Dad replaced my torn dress with two new ones. Arlene never bothered me again. Forgotten? No, it never will be!

"Have you noticed how busy and happy your grandmother has been lately?" Dad asked me.

"Well, Dad, she is always happy when the weather becomes nice," was my nonchalant reply.

"Well, it is more than good weather with her. Your Uncle Chet is bringing Herman home to spend a week with her. She is so excited about having him for a few days. But I don't want you girls around him. He seems harmless, but it has been known that he can show his temper."

Dad was very protective of Sylvia and me, especially about health concerns. He startled me almost out of my skin one evening as I began to tease and pull him from his chair. (It was romp time.) "Get away from my shoes! Never touch my chair when I've just come from the parlor," he shouted at me. "I have been walking on germs for hours." He really scared me. It was the tone of his voice—a sound of terror!

Grandma finally had Herman with her, and what a picture they made sitting together on her porch, Grandma rocking and crocheting while Herman talked and laughed to himself. The rockers on his chair had a time keeping up with his feet. What a grand time they were having. I could feel the contagious, sweet contentment between them, so it was worth taking a chance of breaking Dad's warning about staying away from Herman. Sylvia and I didn't hesitate for a minute. We were up on Grandma's porch as soon as Dad was out of sight. And, as all kids invariably will say when not invited, we asked, "What are you doing?"

Herman's eyes lit up like stars as Grandma replied, "We are having a good rock. As if you didn't know."

We sat there cross-legged for what seemed like hours watching Herman rock. Once, I thought he was going to rock off the porch. "Be careful, Herman!" I warned him.

"Now, Maydeen," he said. He couldn't say Nadine and "Susie Ann" was for Sylvia. He enjoyed us because children brought amusement and pleasure; after all, he was a child in a body of a man. We became his good friends for the next few days because we made him laugh. We loved to sing while he rocked because he would attempt to sing along with us, which was hilarious. We managed to have popcorn every day, and the best treat of all was our delightful walks. We watched and protected him, his hand in ours. He never failed to wear his brown, felt hat or to say, "Good-by, Mamma" before leaving the house. It seemed so strange for my precious grandmother to be referred to as Mamma. I thought several times that I should tell Dad we were with Grandma and Herman, but he was a step ahead of me. "I know you want to tell me that you are spending time with Herman. You don't need to bother. I know all about it, and so does everyone in Dallas. Well, I think your grandmother appreciates a little help. You kids were great getting Herman across the street with no mishap," he said with a chuckle.

I noticed Dad didn't seem to be feeling too well. He wasn't his usual vibrant self. And how I did miss his mischief-making and laughter. One morning his hands shook so hard he nearly dropped his coffee cup. I was also aware that he was using some kind of an eyedrop which caused the outer edge of his eyes to turn a brownish-gold color. When I questioned him about his eyes he would always answer with an "Oh, I'm just a little tired. It is nothing at all. You know, I think it is time we drive over to Garibaldi, and get a breath of that good old salt air. It would be good for all of us." So that very Sunday we drove over to Garibaldi.

Grandmother was delighted to be included. She said several times, "Oh, that ocean air is so good for the soul." I kept wondering just what she meant by that. Aunt Ora and Uncle Kile were elated to have us, especially Aunt Ora. She was so adorable whenever she became excited. I thought so many times that she would make a fitting Mrs. Santa Claus because her round, little body quivered like a bowl of jelly when she became tickled about something. She had a wonderful chicken dinner for us. It was more like a delectable feast. It was sensational in every way, including her luscious rhubarb pie.

Sylvia and I entertained ourselves that afternoon in the lovely woods in the back of their property. I loved it back there, the huge trees, ferns, wildflowers, and that gorgeous, woodsy fragrance. *I could live out here forever,* I thought. Aunt Ora and Dad had a very long visit. It was dusk by the time we reached home since we didn't leave Garibaldi till late afternoon. I was surprised and quite taken back when Dad said, "I have always wanted to see the cherry orchards in bloom, so let's treat ourselves to the sight everyone is raving about." The orchards were just a few miles from Dallas, so it was a short drive. We could see the cherry trees were in full bloom because the March moon cast a bright glow over the entire orchard. The evening dew and the soft, caring breeze made each blossom glisten and dance in the moonlight. Not a word was uttered as Dad drove in and through the trees. We were enamored with what we were seeing, as if we were in a dream. I felt as though Mother Nature had wrapped me in a blanket of magic beauty and love.

The next morning began like every other Monday school day with a hurry-up breakfast, a hurry-up bedmaking, primp, primp, and off to school. I was just leaving by the back door when Dad called to me, "Nadine, I want to talk to you!" I was surprised when he called me from his bedroom, as I thought he had already left for work. I was shocked even more so to see him still in bed, as this never before happened. "Please stand over by the window. I want to see you as clearly as I can. You know, your mother always said this house was too dark."

I did as he requested, but wondered why. As I stood by the long, narrow window, I became chilled with fear. As the sheer, lace curtain blew in through the window, touching me, something about all of this terrorized me. "Now, I am going to talk to you. And I want you to pay close attention to what I am going to say because I am going to die. You and your sister will live with your Aunt Ora. It is all arranged. I am leaving you girls plenty of money for the best of education and to have everything you need." He went on to say that Albert Hawke was the lawyer who had his will.

"Dad, you are not going to die. And Dad, you know you can't trust Albert Hawke." I was beside myself.

"Yes, I am going to die. Now listen to me. Your Uncle Chet was my first choice to take you two girls but with Florence in her condition, he couldn't say yes. Your Aunt Ora will give you a good home. But if ever you need help, go to your Uncle Roy. Most important of all, please stay close to your sister. She is going to need you. That is all I have to say, except that I love you."

I left his room, shouting firmly back at him, "You are not going to die!" I was shaking all over, and my heart was racing like a wildfire until I saw Aunt Florence out in the yard. I was relieved. "Please, call the doctor! Call Uncle Chet, because Dad is dying. Please! We need help!"

I felt hysterical when she said, "Now Nadine, you must calm down. Your dad isn't dying. Go on to school. You'll see that everything is fine with your father."

Grandma was standing out on her porch listening to my pleas for help. "Now, now, you mustn't get so upset. Your Aunt Florence is right. Your dad is fine. So you go along now to school," Grandma said.

I did as they told me, believing I was right. Dad needed help, I knew it. Never before had he spoken about dying. I was pleased to see Joan, my pal, waiting patiently for me at school. My first thought was that she would believe me and maybe help me. Her face turned white with fear, then she said, "Come on, Nadine, let's go to Mr. Bell" (the principal).

I was beginning to feel like a bouncing ball with no one to catch me, but the two of us did find Mr. Bell and I told him the frightening story. He agreed to call Uncle Chet. "Please don't worry, everything will be fine," he assured me, so I did as everyone told me to do—I went on to my classes. But something cold and strange came over me. I thought I was going crazy. My head felt hot. I wanted to scream. I sobbed, not able to stop. The tears kept flowing. My teacher was so alarmed when I cried out, "I must go to my dad," she helped me leave the classroom without hesitation.

I ran as fast and as hard as I could for home. When I flung open the squeaky back screen door, I was alarmed to hear the hum of voices. There was a strong sickening odor which I recognized to be the smell of gunpowder. I knew Dad was gone! Mrs. Hamilton grabbed me and held me tight as I sobbed. Suddenly, I remembered Slyvia would be home any minute for lunch, so I had to get hold of myself. I pulled away from Mrs. Hamilton just in time, because I heard the screeching sound of the screen door. It was Sylvia. I went to her, and as I did so, I led her back outside. With care and compassion and in privacy, I told her that Dad had died and now he was with Mother. "So it is just you and me now." We cried and sobbed together. I remembered Dad asking me to stay close to my sister because she would need me, and then I wondered, *Who is going to be close to me?* I felt so alone. The pain was devastating. The relatives were all stunned and shocked themselves, making it difficult to know what to say or do, and when they were attempting to explain to us as to how our father died, they were astonished and amazed when I said, "I know how Dad died. He shot himself." I had remembered the lingering, offensive odor from his hunting rifle the day his rifle accidentally went off in Mother's kitchen, so it was very obvious to me what had happened.

I thought it quite strange when Mary (Ruth's friend) came to our house. Ruth met her at the door and said, "What are you doing here? Haven't you done enough damage?" Mary left immediately, and Ruth didn't dream that I had overheard her. I kept my "knowing" to myself. Mary's name was never mentioned again.

The next few days were extremely difficult. I felt as though I was in another world—a spooky, strange world. Everyone who spoke, spoke in low tones. And when there was a conversation, it would suddenly come to an end whenever I appeared. Food! I have never seen so much to eat from friends and strangers. Why did they do this, I wondered, when I couldn't eat? It would only go down in lumps. Then there was Suparpie. She was so scared she would not come into the house. I

47

wanted to cuddle her and feel her softness. Finally, the night before Dad's funeral, she came to me and I held her as close to my chest as I dared. I felt her love reach my heart as she snuggled next to me through the night.

I have never been hypnotized, but I imagine the day of Dad's funeral that I had been just that. I felt as though my outer self had been coated with stone, guarding and protecting my inner self. I wanted to cry out but my stone wall kept it all inside. I didn't hear one word of the minister's message, or any part of the military ceremony, but I do recall Sylvia sitting next to me squirming and wiggling. "Sit still and pull your dress down," I whispered to her. Then the soloist began to sing. She sang the same music that was sung for Mother's funeral, which had been only two months earlier. I closed my eyes and my hands covered my ears. I was stunned and so unprepared. I think now, *The nerve of those people!*

Viewing the casket was different for me this time because my eyes were open. I had to see Dad one last time, his face so handsome, so peaceful. As I said good-bye, I touched his strong, beautiful face, not realizing the cold, icy shock it would give me. Aunt Florence grabbed my hand and held it. "I'm sorry, I'm sorry," she said through tears. Since the funeral was a military one, there had to be a twenty-one rifle salute at the burial. I didn't like it. I thought how much Mother would have hated it. My stone wall crumbled. Every shot from the guns seemed to go clear through my body and I trembled while Sylvia pressed herself close to me. I made sure Aunt Florence was next to me. Dad's burial came to an end with his casket lowered down next to Mother's still fresh grave. March 19, 1934, was not only a long, hard day, but one that left my young heart deeply scared.

After the funeral, relatives and close friends gathered at Aunt Florence and Uncle Chet's house, and later drinks and a buffet dinner were served. It seemed as though everyone was there except Uncle Chet. He was still at the office with Albert Hawkes. As far as I knew he never did come home for dinner. Jim and Eunice Hawkes did not come to the gathering and I was baffled by this because they were Sylvia's and my best friends. I wanted with all of my heart to go home with them for a few days. They did not come near us, even at the funeral. I could not comprehend this because I knew they loved Sylvia and me. Then I thought maybe they were just too sad.

As the evening progressed the dinner turned into a more adult feast and party. *Why do they celebrate?* I wondered. Aunt Florence suggested that Ruth take us home. I didn't want to go, but of course I did. Our home had become a very distressful place for me.

The next big step was going back to school. I knew I would be behind with my studies and was dreading that part of my return, but I felt such exhilaration thinking about my school friends that I became excited for the first time in days. *I won't even worry about my studies*, I thought. Somehow things were not as I had expected them to be. Some of my friends would not speak, let alone look at me. When the bell rang for class time, I walked to my schoolroom alone instead of walking with my circle of friends. I felt as though I had done something unspeakable. They must have thought of me as being weird because I didn't have a mother or father. I was not like the other kids. Time was not on my side. I wanted it to go faster, but it wouldn't. The more I squirmed, the slower time went. I didn't think class would ever end. I could also see that I was far behind the other kids with my studies. This brought more negatives to my mind. I was beginning to feel hot and funny inside. I wanted to go home. I didn't say a word to anyone as I jumped up from my desk and ran for home with Mr. Bell behind me

Ruth was thunderstruck as I tore into the house. "I don't know what happened," I remember Mr. Bell saying. I shudder as I think of the strange, bizarre emotion that swept over me. I had to open the closed door to Dad's bedroom. The first thing that I noticed was the open window with the same thin, lace curtains still moving slightly from a breeze. I stood there remembering his last words to me. Then I cried with grief and anger. "How dare you leave us! I hate you! I hate everyone who wouldn't listen to me. Now I guess I'm a freak, a dumb freak." I sobbed while my heart screamed with pain. With tears flowing down my face, I wandered around his room reminiscing while hugging his warm coat next to my face. My eyes fell upon the hideous pistol that took his life. It had been placed on his chest of drawers. I went over and clung to the fragile curtain while my body and spirit wrestled with the reality of grief. Indeed, the whale had me. I was so exhausted from such emotional injury that I fell into a deep sleep with Dad's coat still around me.

When I awakened, Ruth, my good friend, was beside me. She smiled as she said, "Nadine, don't ever be hateful toward your dad. What he did, he did for you girls." Because of Ruth, I learned that it was up to me to be the one with a sunny smile. "This will put your friends at ease. You are going to have to be the brave one. It is your friends who are afraid," she said. She was right. It did work. I held my head high and I wore a smile. Soon my friends became as natural as ever and our friendship proceeded.

Chapter Ten

Regardless of our grief and sadness, it was spring, and what a beautiful one we were having. I wanted to do something that was special, something really different! "How about putting on a show, Ruth?" I said. She responded immediately by saying, "Go ahead. That is a wonderful idea. Anything to keep your sister home." We were all tired of trying to keep track of her. Especially me, because I was the one who had to search for her and bring her home. Sylvia agreed a show would be fun. I kept thinking a musical would be a wonderful way to celebrate spring. I was becoming so excited, and you know, the whale disappeared! Sylvia was the star and Suzanne was the co-star. My show was in the making with two stars and nine other little showgirls.

Aunt Florence had a lovely garden of pink tulips out back, so this gave me the idea of a dance through the tulips by using the then popular song *Tiptoe through the Tulips*. How we worked every day over and over again after school. I taught them everything that I had learned in dance class. They danced and tip-toped through Aunt Florence's tulips until I thought it was right. However, it was a relief that not one tulip was broken, as it took nerve to even go near her garden of tulips.

We had several other numbers but the Tulip dance and *Me and My Shadow* were the two most remembered. Sylvia danced and Suzanne danced as her shadow. It was hilarious in the beginning, as Sylvia kept stepping on Suzanne. When we finally had the dance down pat, it became just as cute as it could be. The girls used garden stakes for canes and old straw hats instead of foxy, black top hats. It was exciting for all of us.

I wanted our show to have special pretty decorations because our musical was quite unique, I thought, so I put my thinking cap on and came up with the idea of making paper lanterns from an old wallpaper sample catalog. We spent hours cutting and gluing the paper into the making of lanterns, then we hung them high and low over the entire back yard. What a surprise it was when Uncle Chet joined us by setting up rows of folding chairs. I was so thrilled that I must have thanked him a dozen times. "Well, you can't have a show without chairs," he said in a cut and dried tone. It was obvious that he wanted to be a part of it, but no one should suspect.

Our show opened with much excitement and flutter. All of the little showgirls came wearing their pretty party dresses. Much to my surprise, Ruth had a card table set up with a large bowl of lemonade. Aunt Florence, Grandma, and Uncle Chet were there early and sitting in the front row, as big as life! I was overwhelmed by watching so many people arriving to see our show. Our back yard was filled with a delightful audience. Even Sugarpie had her special place, neatly snuggled under her laurel shrub. Yes, our show was successful. There wasn't one mistake that I knew about. It was too bad, however, that Ruth didn't make enough lemonade. She was also stunned that so many people came. Aunt Florence said in a very amusing way, "I thought it was a shame the tulips couldn't stay in bloom long enough for the dance. But it was lovely the way the girls danced among the dried-up stems, making the tulips come alive."

The coming of June was not only farewell to my seventh grade, but to my friends, school, and teachers as well. We were preparing to leave Dallas for our new home in Garibaldi. One of the first things on the agenda was to have braces put on my teeth. "You don't want to go through life with crooked teeth," Uncle Chet said. Even though the entire thought scared me stiff, I had to agree with him. Pretending that I was tough and not at all skittish, we walked together up to the dentist's office. I was as straight and forthright as my uncle. I am sure everyone knew we were related. We left the dentist in the same manner except I was the one with the swollen, sore mouth.

Even though he appeared dignified and had such an air of self-assurance, Uncle Chet did display his tender side this day. "In a few days your Aunt Florence and I plan to take you and your sister to Portland to see the Rose Parade and Festival." As he broke this wonderful news to me, he nonchalantly handed me some aspirin. I was so thrilled with this exciting news that I almost forgot about my sore mouth and the aspirin.

I could hardly wait to tell Sylvia about this thrilling news. When I did, her eyes became as big as silver dollars and there were squeals of joy from both of us! The Rose Festival, so wonderful, so exciting! We would get to sleep in a real hotel and eat in restaurants. Then I felt my mouth, wondering if I would ever be able to eat again. But I wasn't any different than most kids, I healed in a hurry. Not only that, we were packed days before we were to leave for Portland. Both of us thought the time would never come. Then I thought that maybe we shouldn't be in such a hurry because Garibaldi would come fast enough without our pushing it. I loved the coast and Aunt Ora was so very special. But leaving our friends and Dallas was hurtful and scary. What would my new friends be like? What if no one liked me? But then the anticipation of the Rose Festival overshadowed the worry I was creating. I knew the parade would be beautiful and exciting. What a joy to see. Ah yes! There was such a feeling of ecstasy.

The Rose Festival was even more beautiful than I had imagined it to be, especially the parade with its huge flower-covered floats. I tingled all over while admiring the gorgeous, very feminine girls in their bouncy, fluffy gowns. And oh, that festival queen, so regal and beautiful. The excitement of seeing and hearing the marching bands made my heart pound with elation. Yes, that year there were two girls watching the parade who were starry-eyed with wonderment of it all!

"I thought it odd when adventurous Sylvia seemed to be a little afraid of the horses, while Nadine looked as though she might jump right in and join them," Aunt Florence said with a chuckle. In one respect she was right. I was dazzled with the beauty of those fabulously decorated Arabian horses. As they pranced and danced down the city street, I felt my chin quiver and my eyes become misty. How magnificent those animals were, and the proud riders had such control and dignity. Well, I was in a world all of my own.

Aunt Florence did quite well walking through the crowds with her cane and, of course, our help. She didn't miss one part of the fun and she never uttered a word of complaint.

We were not expecting to go shopping, but we did, for new clothes. I was completely surprised. And, yes, it wasn't a secret that we both were in need of new clothing. We were not only in need, but we also adored pretty clothes.

There was almost too much happiness all at once. We felt quite grown up and special having our own hotel room next to Aunt Florence and Uncle Chet. But most important of all, I felt secure and cozy as I snuggled up in my blanket for the night, knowing they would be there in the morning. It was a happy, wonderful time—the festival, the streetcar rides, and, of course, the huge stores. It must have been comical and unforgettable for Aunt Florence and Uncle Chet as we both were so mesmerized, especially by the big city restaurants. Never did we turn down a chance to eat!

When we arrived home, I was surprised to see that Ruth had all of our belongings packed, ready for our move to Garibaldi. A box was even waiting for Sugarpie. Everything was ready, except our feelings. I had such mixed up, torn thoughts. I was frightened. If we were unhappy over there we wouldn't have Dad to rescue us, but then I would think, *Dad had to be sure because he said it all was in his will.* "Do you think we will really be all right, Ruth?" I asked her.

"Of course you will. Your Aunt Ora is such a good person, you know that."

Then I said, "Dad told me he put in his will that we were to live with her, so it must be the right thing to do."

A strange expression crossed Ruth's face. Then she surprisingly said, "Will? What will?"

"Dad's will, Ruth. Dad told me that morning Albert Hawke had his will and Sylvia and I had nothing to worry about because Aunt Ora would be taking care of us." I knew immediately Ruth was troubled. And I also sensed this subject should be dropped, so we both went about our affairs.

The next morning, bright and early, we were ready to leave with Uncle Chet and another man. Later I learned that this other man was his lawyer. There were no good-byes, really. However, Grandma and I did exchange weak, sorrowful waves. Aunt Florence didn't do too well and had tears in her eyes. Ruth said, "You'll be just fine." If I had only known this was the last time I would ever see her again, she would have had more from me than just a simple good-bye. She was such an important friend of mine. Well, there we were, packed in, not too snugly, into the back seat with Sugarpie disapproving and grumbling in the middle. Sylvia and I sat as though we were two marble statues. Not a word or a whisper did we utter.

Chapter Eleven

Aunt Ora and Uncle Kile were waiting for us and expressed such happy enthusiasm upon our arrival. I gave a big sigh of relief when Uncle Kile took Sugarpie from her box in such a gentle, tender way and then helped Sylvia and me with the rest of our belongings. Aunt Ora was having what seemed to be an important discussion with Uncle Chet and the lawyer. I knew it was about us. They didn't stay long, and when they did leave, it was with a cold, informal good-bye. I was glad when they left because Uncle Chet was entirely different while he was with this man.

Our first day was a quiet one, a "get acquainted day," if you will, of our new comfy, lived-in home, which always had a beautiful aroma of homemade bread. Aunt Ora cooked and baked on a handsome, shiny, wood range. Believe me, no one could outdo her pies, cinnamon rolls, or other baked goods. She gave all of the credit to her delightful oven! I truly believed nothing would ever fail, not in that magic oven of hers. We were also thrilled with our delightful new room with a gorgeous view of the bay. What a sight it was during sunset. While we were both busy and enjoying the task of unpacking and putting away our things, Sugarpie had found her new place of comfort and security curled up on my bed. Oh! Sweet essence! She was one happy cat!

Even though we were comfortable and pleased with it all, there was a deep feeling of loneliness that overcame me. I felt so far away from everyone. The rain, dark clouds, and the coast mist caused heavy-heartedness for both of us. We had to do something to create our own sunshine. This we surely did. One day I discovered how dry it was under Uncle Kile's loganberry arbor. It was just high enough for us to be comfortable underneath, so we spent time under the berry arbor building houses, roads, and stores for our paper dolls. We ended up having a make-believe community of rock gardens and miniature flower gardens. They were artistic and so adorable. What marvelous contentedness we had created. Sugarpie soon learned that she had her own spot. She didn't dare look as though she might step on a blossom or sit on a house. Aunt Ora and Uncle Kile were smart to leave us to our own visualization at this time. We did, however, expect Aunt Ora to scold us for snitching so many of her fuchsia blooms, but there was never a cross word.

When the weather had broken and the sun finally decided to show its glory, Uncle Kile took us to the ocean and the beach, and then to my most favorite place in the world—my lake! Aunt Ora had decided it was time we should make friends, but we were too shy, or maybe we just were not ready. Instead we both were charmed and, yes, fascinated by the wooded mountain behind Uncle Kile's chicken yard and garden—the old fir and pine trees, gorgeous green moss, wildflowers. And wow!, those bright red huckleberries. No one could lose us because we left a trail of paper doll settlements which had green moss lawns. We were busier than ever. Sugarpie was beside herself with all of the new smells and adventures. She was fun to watch. We had our own enchanted refuge. The haunting, lonely, screeching noise from the gulls and the crows suddenly, as if overnight, became uplifting and refreshing, as if from tears to laughter.

We now were ready for the excitement of watching the big truck tug and groan up the steep hill to our house with Mother's pride and joy—the piano. Uncle Chet had sent the instrument to us. Both Sylvia and I were intoxicated with excitement and with the thrill of seeing and touching the old piano. I suddenly became at home in Garibaldi! What a glorious feeling of wholeness. My heart was peaceful. How amazing it was, our old friend the piano. Our music eventually brought friends to us, boys and girls alike. It was as though they had always been there, only waiting for the right time to be known.

Swimming in the lake, walking in the woods, climbing around on the jetty rocks, and the excitement of clam-digging made this a summer overflowing with enjoyment. The endearing times spent in the quiet of Uncle Kile's garden was wonderful. We never carelessly walked or spoke in a loud manner, only in a soft tone, or even a whisper. Perhaps we feared we would disturb a growing plant or seed. It was a beautiful garden with the blackest, richest sandy soil ever seen. I called it "Uncle Kile's Heavenly Garden."

Aunt Ora and Uncle Kile's closest friends were the Garrisons from Texas. He was a big man who wore tweed suits; a beige Stetson hat; and smoked huge, long cigars. He was a retired attorney, and she had been a nurse. I remembered her helping Aunt Ora care for Mother. At the time, I thought she was rather strange—almost spooky. She portrayed herself as being quite austere and disapproved of anyone who might be having fun. Her snow-white hair intrigued me because never was there a hair out of place, even during our constant ocean breeze. My puzzle was solved the day I spotted a silver hairnet protecting her precious white hair. *Ah ha*, I thought. Her skin was as white as her hair, with traces of white powder. Her house was absolutely pure and simple, with an aroma of caramel. I learned later that she would burn sugar to destroy offensive food odors. *Poor Mr. Garrison*, I would think. *How could he ever be permitted to light one of his delectable cigars?* Yes, the Garrisons were frequent visitors at our house, so we would find excuses to busy ourselves elsewhere, such as going up to see the Vogts.

The Vogts lived up at the top of our hill in a lovely English stucco house, but most important, it was a friendly home, and we were always welcomed there by Mr. and Mrs. Vogt and their three offspring. Bob, the oldest, was a law student; Ruth was in the middle, and a junior in high school; Doug would be a freshman the coming year. They were big people with hearts to match. Now, Doug had elected himself to be my big protector and advisor. There were so many "do's" and "don'ts" regarding the coast and woods. "By the way, you shouldn't be climbing those trees in back of your house. The limbs are weak and brittle," he said.

"How do you know we climb trees?" I asked him.

"Cause I see you with my binoculars," he said with a ho-ho.

Well, we should have listened, because the very next day a limb cracked and broke with me on it and I fell to the ground, knocking myself out. When I came to my senses, I saw Sylvia standing over me, her mouth wide open and her eyes as big as dollars. "Why didn't you get me help, dummy?" I asked her.

"Because, I thought you were dead," was her reply. Of course that set like a lead balloon.

Believe me, Doug didn't help my bruised self and especially my ego when he said, "I told you so!"

"You give me those binoculars, Doug Vogt!" I ordered him. He just laughed and went on his merry way.

We were both ready for school that fall even though the thought was somewhat scary. "A new adventure," I said to Sylvia so many times that I came to believe it myself. The so-called adventure was a complete surprise; it was almost a shock to be greeted with so much fondness and to be already known. It was wonderful! My new classmates were inviting me into a world of friendship. I felt like whirling and dancing, as my heart was overflowing with jubilation.

Dad would have been proud of me, because right away and with enthusiasm I joined the band with my saxophone. Neil Huckleberry, another eighth grader, became a band member with his small version of a tuba. The band consisted mainly of high school students. My saxophone was an alto, so Neil and I were selected to do the oom-pah-pah's. Needless to say, we both would become tickled and often came down with a bad case of giggles. Poor Mr. Dunn, the band instructor, the patience he must have had. Neil was one of my best friends. His bright red hair and freckles made a charming picture, framing his terrific sense of humor. He was a ray of sunshine. His peppy, vivacious mother was very likable and always busy and interested in everything that pertained to our community, especially with the kids. She was a real doer; I liked her immediately. How pleased I was when she invited me to their home for a party. Nothing really special, just a party. There were games of all kinds, all of them were such fun! I had to do some imitations, which came fairly easy for me as we had imitated different actors with Dad. I loved doing Jimmy Durante; Mae West; and my favorite, Zazu Pitts. The kids nearly died laughing. The rest of the evening was spent just being silly until Mrs. Huckleberry served ice cream and cake, which always was a special treat and created a happy ending for any kid's party. By that time Dr. Huckleberry, who was a quiet, impressive man, had arrived home just in time to bid farewell to all of us. My first party came and went with a happy ending.

My eighth grade in Garibaldi was a good one. I felt as though I had joined one big family. Not once did I think of myself as being a stranger. While the weather was still good we would often hike down to the Barview Lake after school for a swim. This was a marvelous release for me! Regardless of the fun and enjoyment of school, there would be emotional suffering for me. I wanted so much to let Dad and Mother know we were all right. I was so lonely for them, especially at evening time. I didn't realize but I know today that my love for the water eased my hurt. Many times I would go to the lake alone and swim to my heart's content. It seemed unusual that many of my new friends were poor swimmers or they didn't know how to swim at all, especially since they lived at the beach. It didn't make sense to me at all. It is no wonder the lake was known as "Nadine's Lake."

The school was up at the top of our hill and then over a few blocks. We were lucky to be within walking distance so we could come home for Aunt Ora's special lunches. Many times she would have clam chowder and always homemade bread. She enjoyed cooking for us because we thought of her as the best cook in the world! I do not recall her ever scolding or being angry. Nor did she ever appear to worry. We could do almost everything we wanted to do.

It seemed rather astounding to me that she so seldom ever mentioned Uncle Chet's name, especially after one particular visit. There was a disagreement, I was sure of that, because Mrs. Garrison was obviously telling him what was what, then he left for home in a big huff! As he drove away in anger, Aunt Ora was distraught. I was sure of that. I felt certain it all was because of Sylvia and me, so I said, "Aunt Ora, we don't need to worry because it is in Dad's will that we live here with you."

"There is no will. It seems to have disappeared," she said. Of course this was upsetting to me, but since this episode was not discussed any further, I concentrated on my private concerns, especially my studies, the band, and the fun times. I had been selected from our band to play a saxophone solo at a Bay City banquet. *This is really neat*, I thought. No one from school attended the banquet except Mr. Dunn and me. I played *Melody of Love* and must have done all right as I had an encore— I was invited back. I remember being so tickled because, even with braces on my teeth, my saxophone reed didn't squeal once. I prayed so hard the night before, "Please, God, keep my saxophone from making a squeal, oh please!" He must have heard my emotional plea. I remembered Mother saying, "Always say thank you, especially to God." I thanked him more than once!

This was the winter Garibaldi would never forget, the 1935 Year of the Snow! It snowed and snowed some more. We didn't think it would ever stop. We almost went crazy with the excitement of it because it is a rarity for the coast to ever be touched by that white magic from heaven. We were all delighted and, as you can imagine, our steep hill had become a very popular place for the kids. No one in Garibaldi owned an elegant, store-bought sled, so everyone I knew was creating and building their own. I might add there were some of the strangest sleds ever invented, plus big tin lids, anything that would slide. Bob and Doug really helped the sliding situation by hosing down the road. No one was in need of a sled after that. If you just looked at the hill of ice you'd slide. That night our hill resembled a sparkling, crystal jewel! So beautiful.

Mr. Vogt and the boys built the largest bonfire I had ever seen up at their house, where we roasted hot dogs and marshmallows. Later Mrs. Vogt, bless her heart, busied herself by making hot chocolate for all of the kids. There must have been close to thirty-five young people. How good everything was, and the fun. My face hurt, not from the cold, but from laughing. The peak of the evening was when Doug let me ride on the back of his sled, that is, if I would promise to hang on tight and not let go. "I promise, I promise!" I said. It is a good thing I didn't let go or I might not be here today. Wow! What a thrill! I felt as though I had left part of myself up at the top of the hill. I hugged myself, making sure that this was real, not imagined. Tonight was a kid's fanciful winter dream come true, not a pretend illusion.

Walking to and from school often became a challenge. I am referring to the southwestern coastal storms. We never knew in those days when one might descend upon us; however, we were warned many times about dangers and to never touch a fallen electrical wire. Believe me, there were many times when we had to walk around a downed wire! It was quite common to hear the cracking and crashing sound of falling trees. The experience was frightening for us at first, but in time we found it to be fun to be pushed by the wind, and how hilarious it was to have my umbrella blow wrong-side out. I pretended it was a parachute. I felt smart wearing my knee-high rubber boots like the other kids did. I soon found it to be exhilarating, the wind and the rain! Aunt Ora, with Sugarpie, would be watching for us, and relieved when we were in sight. She always had towels ready for our sopping, drenched heads. How wonderful the fire felt from her trusty, beautiful wood range.

The storms at night appeared more vicious, so dark and mysterious. The groaning, growling painful sounds from the trees were unbearable as the wind continued to attack. One huge pine tree fell from the powerful wind into Uncle Kile's chicken yard, crushing the chicken house. Much damage was done, especially to Uncle Kile's pride and joy—his chickens! No, I could never keep the fear from my heart when suddenly a southwestern storm would rage at night. It would remind me of a whirling, whistling ghost touching and swaying our house. Many times we could feel our bed move, as its old fashioned coasters were not stable. I would shut my tear-filled eyes and wonder what brave words Dad would say to us. "Shut your eyes. Go to sleep, because a calm, peaceful morning will be here before you know it." Yes, I am sure that is what Dad would have said.

We were happy and relieved when winter weather was becoming less fierce and small signs of spring were beginning to appear, so Uncle Kile became very busy preparing his garden soil for planting and pondering over his almanac, which was his garden bible. He never sowed a seed without consulting his faithful almanac, but I felt my Uncle Kile was the best weatherman there ever was. More than once he would say, "You better get yourself in. It is going to rain soon."

"How do you know, Uncle Kile?" I would ask.

"Well now, see the smoke from my pipe. It is going away from the west, so it is going to rain."

All I could say was, "Gee, that is great!" He never worked outside without his pipe. From then on, I was fascinated with that intriguing pipe of his.

"Ora, I'm concerned about the eggs under both of those setting hens. It is going to be cold tonight," Uncle Kile said. So they both decided it would be wise to bring the eggs inside. Aunt Ora carefully placed them in a cardboard box and pushed the box full of eggs under her wood range, where it was nice and warm. This was the day before Easter and our plans were to go to church decked out in our new Easter outfits and then have a luscious ham dinner, topped off with lemon pie. Of course, Uncle Kile was right as always about the weather. It was a miserable cold and rainy morning so our Easter dresses were not quite so exciting as they should have been. We came downstairs in a disgruntled mood. "Why does it always have to rain?" I asked.

"There is lots of sunshine in the kitchen, girls," Aunt Ora said. "Just look!" she exclaimed. I couldn't believe my eyes. There were baby chicks all over Aunt Ora's kitchen! Some of them were still in the process of hatching. What a sight this Easter morning! Those adorable fluffy, gold, chirping chicks. *Isn't God wonderful to do this just for us?* I thought. They were so fragile and soft. Aunt Ora placed a tiny chick into my cupped hands and I could feel its fast little heartbeat. My emotion of joy became so overwhelming that my heart not only sang but danced with happiness. I was in heaven. This was and had been my favorite Easter through my lifelong years.

The low and high tides were a constant topics of conversation to all who lived in Garibaldi. Of course, high tides brought the excitement and breathtaking exhilaration of the surf. I learned to have respect and reverence for the ocean, as its every wave would be filled with such enormous energy and power, depleting me of my own strength. I very soon would become unlively and weary. Aunt Ora would say, "You are as limp as an old rag." All of my enthusiasm and vigor was somewhere other than in me. The next time the energy; laughter; and, yes, the low tides would be just as exciting, but in a different way. They would bring feelings of expectation and wonderment. I will never forget one special low tide that thrills me as much today as it did while experiencing it. Aunt Ora and Uncle Kile talked about the coming event days before it happened. "The bay may be gone entirely. It should be the most memorable clam harvest for years to come." Every family in Garibaldi was ready for it, me included. Uncle Kile had two buckets and a small shovel ready for my use. The alarm clock was set. I couldn't imagine the bay being gone! It was difficult to sleep. I must have spent most of the night walking back and forth from my bed to view the bay from my window. It was so hard to believe it would be gone.

It was a miracle! That was the only way I could describe my feeling as the morning was breaking and I found myself walking on the wet floor of the bay. All of these people were in absolute silence while clams were squirting with every step taken upon the sand. I began digging as fast as I could with my shovel, but before long, I was on my knees and digging with my hands. It was much faster. My buckets were full in no time at all, so my friends handed me a spare gunny sack to fill. Needless to say, I had to have help going home with all of the clams. Aunt Ora couldn't believe her eyes. She laughed for days while I suffered from a brutal sunburn.

There was sadness this spring. Grandmother passed away. It was said she died from a broken heart. I remember feeling and thinking that everyone dies and leaves me. I wondered, *How many times can a heart be broken?* No one but Grandma called me honeybun. I liked that. How I would miss her.

This was the first time since we moved to Garibaldi that the family came together, and I sensed that there was an ugly, cool attitude toward Aunt Ora. I couldn't understand why. Aunt Florence was the only one who showed compassion and was charming to everyone.

I was dreading the funeral and the sadness it surely would bring. I was worrying also about being in the same room with Uncle Frank and Aunt Ada. I wished it all could be over. My concerns were needless, however, as they both completely avoided me. Uncle Chet had his problems regarding what to do about Herman. He finally decided that it would be best for Herman to attend his mother's funeral, so this he did. We all went together to the funeral and, as hard as I tried not to cry, when Herman sobbed and cried for his mamma, I could not control my tears. I hurt so for Herman. And, oh yes, for myself! We were the only two who cried for Grandma.

After the funeral was over and just before we were to leave for home, Aunt Florence called to me, "I have something for you." It was the precious, pink candy dish that Grandma kept her peppermints in for me. Aunt Florence said that I was the one who should have this dish, as I would enjoy taking care of it for Grandma until I had my own home. I was so elated to have this adorable candy dish. The memories it holds are so dear and beautiful.

My senses were right! There was trouble brewing in the family! Uncle Chet wanted Sylvia and me to move back to Dallas and live with him and Aunt Florence. We were devastated and confused. What right did he have? We were to make our home with Aunt Ora. Everyone must know this! I was frightened, and yet I was quite angry also. I understood he was planning on taking Aunt Ora to court if she wouldn't give us up. "The only reason he wants you two girls is to have control of your money. He will put you both in a strict girls' school. It will be just like a prison. He has no intentions of making a home for you." I was scared. Dad said to me that if ever I needed advice or help, "Go to your Uncle Roy." How could I do that when he, too, was against Aunt Ora? Aunt Ora was not about to send us back to Dallas. The next step was to go to court. We only had a few weeks to prepare for the trial, so Aunt Ora, I might add, with the help of Mrs. Garrison, contacted a prominent lawyer in Tillamook. I felt more confident now and had more determination to face Uncle Chet's opposition. I knew we should win because I felt very positive that the right was on our side. Uncle Chet wished for us to spend a few days with him and Aunt Florence before the trial. He wanted to talk with us. The lawyer for Aunt Ora said, "Absolutely not! She must hide the girls. He can't take them if he doesn't know where they are. Keep them there just a day before the trial."

Our neighbors knew of an excellent hide-out and Aunt Ora and her lawyer agreed it would be good for us to go with this helpful neighbor to the secret place. The neighbors took us in their car. We were on the floor of their car, covered with a blanket so that no one would see us. To this day, I do not know where we were, only that we went through Tillamook because the neighbor made a comment, "Well, there is Roy Henkle and his friends obviously keeping an eye out for you girls." We drove for a long time before we felt secure enough to come out from under the blanket. I was surprised and amazed to find myself up in the mountains. We were in the center of a logging camp. The neighbors then took us to a beautiful log home where we were introduced to the family. They were most friendly and, because they were understanding parents, they knew how to make us feel comfortable and welcome. Immediately we had two new friends, a girl and a boy near our ages. Almost immediately we were running, laughing, and having a wonderful time in this hardy, rugged forest with our two new friends. It was exciting and adventurous. Time went fast for us and before we realized, it was time for dinner, which was served in a big room with the loggers included. They were lighthearted, jovial, and full of humor. I found it fun to only be a good listener. Even their teasing and joshing was enjoyment for me. Amazing for one who was so worried and full of anxiety just a few hours before!

The morning of the next day began as though we were in an imaginary, mystical world. The forest was too beautiful, I thought, to be real. Never had I heard so many birds sing at one time. What sweet, pure music I was hearing! And the never forgotten sun's rays dancing from tree to tree uncovered a very secretive hiding deer. I was spellbound with all of this pleasured magic while running through the ribbons of sunlight. Then, taking time to enjoy the sheer, delectable fragrance of pine, I felt nothing but happiness until minutes later when my world became one of terror. We had decided to play follow the leader through the woods. It was fun and exciting, especially while crossing over a twenty-five-foot wild rapid waterfall on a moss-covered log. Three of us carefully made it across the falls but as I glanced back at Sylvia, I saw her feet slip, then heard her screams. The next horrible sight was her limp body sprawled out down on the river rocks. She wasn't moving, made not a sound. I went crazy. I became hysterical with fear. Was she alive? Help did come, but it took like what seemed to be forever to bring her back up to where we could take her to the Tillamook hospital.

I calmed down when I could see she was alive, but of course no one knew how grave her injuries were. She was dazed, bleeding, and already we could see signs of severe bruising. I was relieved and thankful that Aunt Ora and Uncle Kile were waiting for us at the hospital. We were there for some time as the doctors gave her a detailed examination. How thrilled and how thankful we were when we were told that she was all right. Sylvia was indeed blessed, as a deer, just days before, had fallen down the falls, only to have his neck broken.

This accident happened on a Saturday afternoon and the trial was to begin the following Monday morning. Sylvia could not go because of her injuries, but perhaps it was just as well. The Tillamook Courthouse was conspicuously new and beautiful. It was a brand new courthouse and our trial was one of the first to take place in the new, grand building. I was in awe of it, yet my heart felt a pang of fear and alarm as I entered the solemn, dignified courtroom with Uncle Kile and Aunt Ora.

Why can't we get along? I thought. Down deep I loved them all and I wanted to cry because of it, but dear Judge Meyers had a smile every time our eyes would meet. This was a comfort. However, there was an air about the attorneys, including Mr. Botts, our lawyer, that aggravated me. I resented being referred to as the "said minor." It was as though I didn't have a name, and some of the questions they asked were very upsetting, especially when Aunt Ora's character and honesty were being questioned regarding financial charges to our estate. We were paying her room and board, which I didn't know about, and didn't care. Many of her friends testified on her behalf. They all said she was a good, caring woman, and how much she loved "these two girls."

But then there was the other side. "She is only interested in the girls' money and she is bleeding the estate. The girls won't have enough money left for their education if this kind of spending continues. She doesn't care about the girls' future, she only cares about the money." These words tore through me with agonizing disbelief. Or should I have believed them? *Uncle Roy was standing by his brother instead of his sister, and Uncle Roy wouldn't hurt anyone,* I was thinking as I sat there listening and wondering. I wanted to stand up and shout, "Just stop this!" Then came the vicious opposition against Uncle Chet. "He doesn't want the girls, he only wants control of them and their money. He will take them and then send them away to a boarding school. Florence, his wife, is a cripple. How can she look after two young girls?"

I was hearing too many times, "They don't want you, they only want your money." My hurt was developing into a defensive hate. How dare they not want my beautiful sister and me. We hadn't hurt anyone. Judge Meyers was watching me and not smiling. Uncle Chet's drinking was mentioned several times during the trial and it was said he wasn't fit to have children in his home. I knew he drank and I guess that was bad, I thought, so my feelings at times were torn. Uncle Chet testified that Fred Thomas approached him first before asking anyone else and asked, "if I would consider taking the girls if something were to happen to him. But I didn't take him at all seriously, or I would have said yes, I would. I realize my wife is a cripple, but we still can manage nicely with the help we have. My wife has always been very fond of these two girls. She loves them very much." I wanted to cry with the thought, *Maybe someone really does want us.* He went on talking, describing his big beautiful house. He showed great interest in taking us on trips at his expense and he also expressed a desire for us to attend St. Helen's Hall, a girls' school in Portland. Our education was extremely important to him, and college was a must.

"My wife and I feel strongly that the girls are running wild over there. Nadine spends almost as much time in the lake as she does in school. There is no supervision there whatsoever. We don't like hearing about them running on the beach and walking on the railroad tracks to Barview without an adult. Ora doesn't care about their welfare, and this last episode of hiding the girls in that logging camp just so I couldn't spend time with them was insidious. Sylvia could have been killed. All Ora wants is her monthly paycheck. She doesn't care about the girls, or she would be looking after them much better."

Many Dallas people testified in his behalf as Ora's friends also did for her: "Chet is interested in the money, Ora cares only about her paychecks."

These rash, degrading statements rang in my ears. *No one wants us. No one wants us!* I thought. I felt as though my body was shrinking, and I wanted to hold my hands over my ears. I became nauseous and lightheaded and Judge Meyers dismissed the proceedings until the next morning.

I was prepared to face the throws of the trial the next morning, determined to be brave in the face of diversity. Aunts and uncles be damned! I am me! When I was called to the stand, I decided I was through being thought of as "the said minor," so I did not move from my chair when I was called to testify, and I said, "My name is Nadine Thomas." There were tee-hees throughout the courtroom. When order was restored, I went to the stand after finally being addressed as "Nadine Thomas." In a very feisty manner, I said, "Thank you." Dad would have been proud of me standing up for my rights, and I could almost hear my sweet mother saying, "I'm so pleased you remembered to say thank you!"

I felt unprotected, small, and very alone as I observed the crowded courtroom of serious faces. I was about to give my testimony, knowing it was the most important one to be given. I would think before I spoke, even though my heart was pounding. Mother had wondered if I would ever learn this valuable lesson of hers. I feared I would have a difficult time telling about the last conversation with my father, but my needed courage came. My throat suddenly lost that big lump, and my voice didn't quiver. Sounding bold, my voice became clear and strong. I wanted the world to know my father did have a will and Albert Hawke, a Sheridan lawyer, was in care of it. I was anxious for the court to know Dad wanted Aunt Ora to make a home for Sylvia and me. I love my home in Garibaldi, and I didn't want to leave. I was on the stand for what seemed like hours defending my home and all of my wonderful times and friends who always seemed to be watching out for us. Not once did I feel I was in danger. When asked about Aunt Florence, I expressed my love for her. She was always there for me and would even mend my dolls, but I didn't really know my Uncle Chet well enough to want to live in his house. He and my father had disagreements, and I didn't like that.

Uncle Chet's lawyer was persistent with his questions about my walking from Garibaldi to Barview on the railroad tracks, and of course the swimming in that deep lake without a lifeguard there. "You really don't think that is safe, do you?" he questioned.

"Well," I said, "if you think it is hoboes that I should be afraid of, well, there aren't any hoboes in Garibaldi! I'm a good swimmer, sir, and we don't have lifeguards here, either. One thing about accidents at the beach comes from valley people, sir. Uncle Kile says before every summer begins, 'Well, it's time for the accidents to begin. The stupid valley folks will soon be rolling in.' You see, we people who live over on the coast have a lot of respect for the lakes and ocean." I was stunned by the snickers and giggles that were heard from the courtroom spectators. I was not intending for my statement to be funny and this bothered me.

It was the truth, so the opposition discontinued this line of questioning. Being a naïve fourteen-year-old, I felt hurt inside. "What else besides swimming do you like in Garibaldi?" I was asked.

"I liked playing in the band, and when the tide is low, it becomes great fun digging for clams. I'm good at it too, but not as good as Joe Whitewash. He knows where the clams are the thickest, and the best. We try to find his secret places but we lose him every time."

"Joe Whitewash, is that his real name?" asked the attorney.

"No, it isn't. Everyone calls him Joe Whitewash because he whitewashes everything. His tiny house, and fence, and even his wheelbarrow that he puts his clams in, also are whitewashed. He sells his clams from his wheelbarrow. I belong to the Four-H Club, too, and I am learning a few things about sewing."

"Well, you are a busy girl," said the Dallas lawyer. Then he asked me, "What do you want to be when you grow up?"

"I want to be a singer. I love to sing more than anything else. Mother said many times, 'God gave you a special gift, that singing voice of yours, and you must use it'."

"Do you take music lessons, Nadine?" the Dallas lawyer questioned.

"No, there isn't a music teacher in Garibaldi. But that is okay because I pretend that I am a famous singer, and I sing almost every chance I get. We have my mother's piano, you know, and that is so nice. It makes singing even more exciting and fun."

The subject was changed. "Tell me Nadine, does your Uncle Kile ever drink hard liquor?"

I had to think hard for a few minutes, then I remembered. "Oh yes, one time I remember. It was last Easter he and Mr. Garrison had blackberry wine during dinner, and while grace was being said they both got the giggles. I think it was because Aunt Ora almost tripped over one of the baby chicks. That is the only time I ever saw Uncle Kile have a drink."

I wanted so much to sound grown up with admirable fortitude, but I am positive my voice was more like that of a child. I was weary, and I felt anxious and touchy. I would have enjoyed having a good old-fashioned temper tantrum. I didn't dare.

"Nadine, do you think it was right for your Aunt Ora to hide you away from your uncle?" asked the Dallas lawyer.

"I don't know if it was right." I snapped. "All I know for sure is that we don't want to go to Dallas. But now I wish we could have gone because Sylvia wouldn't have had that awful accident. Do you know, sir, I thought for a while she was going to die." My words brought a long stretch of silence through the spacious but still crowded courtroom. I sensed the sadness and empathy which filled the huge room. All the while, I was struggling for tranquillity and composure. Finally, I continued with my testimony. "If all of my aunts and uncles could get along, none of this would have happened. My wonderful grandmother, they say, died of a broken heart. This would have hurt her even more."

Judge Meyers spoke to the lawyers. "This young girl is to be dismissed. She has gone through enough. Nadine, you did just fine."

The trial was over and in a few days the judge had make his decision. We were to stay with our Aunt Ora. We were so relieved and happy. Now we could go on with our lives.

I wondered, *Where do we go from here?* My heart was full of agonizing, emotional questions. Were we not wanted? I felt dejected. Even though the trial was over, we were hurt—Sylvia with her cuts and bruises and me with my broken heart. Of course, there was a healing and in a short time Sylvia was as good as new. My heart, well, a broken heart can't heal without a scar. If I had heard "I love you" or a compassionate pat or a loving kiss, the scar would not have been so deep. My emotions were like being on a merry-go-round for weeks after the trial, even though the outcome was what I had wished for and wanted. I wondered about Uncle Roy, because Dad had said, "Go to your Uncle Roy if ever you need help." He must have thought Uncle Chet was in the right and Aunt Ora was wrong. If only I could have visited with Aunt Florence once in awhile or if I could just have seen Uncle Roy, but Aunt Ora would never permit such a thing. I did remember that Dad asked Uncle Chet first to take us. Of course, he hadn't thought Dad was serious. My mind was in a whirl and I wondered about Albert Hawke. What had he done with Dad's will?

Thank the good Lord for my friends, though there were times I didn't treat them too well. A neighbor girlfriend came by to see me and I insulted her and I asked her to leave, thinking she didn't want to visit with me anyway. Why would she? My music was a pleasure until a mistake was made. *It is no wonder that no one wants me. I can't do anything right,* I thought. There was no doubt about it. I was in a deep depression. I enjoyed going out into Uncle Kile's garden and I deliberately pulled up carrots and green onions, then I left them to spoil. I felt so ugly inside I wanted everyone else to suffer right along with me.

Aunt Ora and I had a heated argument this day and I left the house in a nasty huff for the lake. Disagreements were many these days, but this time I must have taken the right action because as soon as my body touched the cool, fresh water I felt a gentle relief. My thoughts became soothed and unruffled. I could hear the pounding sound of the hidden surf from behind the lake's steep sand hill as I swam. I adored listening and swimming to the rhythm of this powerful energy. There were times the surf made hurtful sounds, as though raging, blasts of anger. The next day the surf would often be completely opposite with fun-loving, wistful rhythm, almost a feeling of playful mischief. Today was like none other. The waves were lazy and slow with a soft and endearing melodious strain. As I swam and swam, a beautiful sensation of love came and caressed me. My entire body from the top of my head to the tip of my toes became filled with complete happiness as my tears of joy mingled with the water of the lake. The cool water became warm with self love, and I wallowed in it. I knew everything in my life was as it should be. It was okay! Everything was okay! I left the lake with a glorious, exciting song in my heart. I gave the old whale a whopper of a smile as I left him there in the lake. Instead of a weary mile-hike back home, it became a frisky, carefree one on this happy, special day.

Aunt Ora greeted me with a plate of hot, delicious cinnamon rolls, as only she could make, as I arrived at the back door. She chuckled as she encouraged me to take more than just one. The quarrel we had was never mentioned again, nor were the many other disagreeable episodes. We went about out lives for the rest of the summer on a happy note.

Chapter Twelve

When the end of August arrived, every adult and kid began looking forward to the Tillamook County Fair, and we were no exception. The wild rides and the carnival always brought a sparkle to our eyes. The exhibits were all right but not exciting except to the older people. The shows were more interesting, but not at all as fun as the rides. Our Four-H Club was planning a booth. I had a dress Aunt Ora had made (instead of myself) and I was to display it and also wear it during a style show. I was not at all enthused about this event, but how elated and excited I was with Uncle Kile's marvelous sunflower. In fact, everyone in Garibaldi was watching it with great interest. It was huge. It seemed as though every day the flower would get bigger and bigger. I thought a giant should own it because it was so tall. We all knew it would win a blue ribbon!

The night before Uncle Kile was to take the sunflower to the fairgrounds, Sylvia decided it would be even more special if she carved her initials into the flower. There she was, up on a stepladder just finishing her artwork, when I heard Aunt Ora's screams! Sylvia was so startled and shocked she almost fell from the ladder. Uncle Kile was so angry that he could not speak. He turned pale and shook! Our dinner table that evening was in complete silence. I remember Sugarpie even stayed outside.

The fair was as spectacular as ever. We often heard, "I do believe the fair gets better each year." I agreed while enjoying my own kind of fun, even if a certain sunflower was missing. I wore and modeled my Four-H dress, which won a ribbon. Much to my surprise, a picture of me wearing it was taken for the newspaper. "Wait till Chet and Florence see this!" Aunt Ora exclaimed.

"You made the dress Aunt Ora." I was disgusted and I am sure she sensed my disfavor. It was a good-looking dress all right, but I seldom wore it.

Fall was nearly here. For those who don't know, I must say that this is the most beautiful time of year at the coast. Everyone who lives there will agree. More picnics and parties are given now than at any other time. That fall for me was more than just special because I was going to be a freshman in high school! All of my classmates were as elated and thrilled as I was. And how wonderful—a big beach party had been planned just for the freshman right down next to the surf. I was so excited that I couldn't stand still as we all lined up and tightly grasped hands so that we could jump the breakers together. It was the most exhilarating fun I had ever experienced. I laughed and screamed until I was completely exhausted. I was not too tired, however, to eat and enjoy the roasted hot dogs and mustard, even though the mustard was gritty with sand. My hands trembled from the aftershock of the icy, cold surf.

Now, finally, I am one of the big kids, I was thinking this special morning as I left for school. I was all decked out in a grown-up skirt and sweater and toting my grave, important briefcase. I felt superior and proud. I not only walked with assurance but expressed my haughtiness as well. However, my balloon was soon to burst. I had no idea that freshman were considered inferior. We were the bottom-most, according to the upperclassmen. *Well, that is okay,* I thought. I had lots of company, as the freshman stayed close to one another.

My day was progressing quite well. I liked all of my teachers and my classes held my attention. I felt pleased with all of it in spite of the high and mighty upperclassmen, Doug included. It wasn't until late morning while sitting at my desk that I began to feel odd, so hot and weak. My stomach was cramping. I kept thinking that it would go away and that it probably was just nerves, but it wasn't going away and I could feel perspiration rolling off of me and the pain in my stomach was excruciating. I wanted to cry, it was so painful. I was frightened because I thought something horrible was happening to me. The next thing I remember was Doug taking me home, so I unknowingly must have passed out. Aunt Ora put me to bed with a hot water bottle. By evening I was fine. Aunt Ora explained to me that it was nothing more than monthly cramps. I had never before heard of this. "That cold ocean water the day before didn't do you a bit of good," she said. So I did learn something else that day besides school. I was very modest and, yes, embarrassed over this incident. Of course, Doug had fun teasing me about my pea-green complexion. The teasing was good. With this dash of humor, my embarrassment was soon forgotten.

School was a sanctuary from summer and I had an eagerness for it. Perhaps this is why it was such a wonderful school year! I enjoyed all of my teachers and subjects. Since I had not lost my enthusiasm for basketball, I made the team in spite of being a freshman and being "short on one end," as they say. Our girls' team was considered as important as the boys' in those days. We played serious, hard ball. There was stiff competition up and down the coast. We traveled to the games in a tiny school bus, which was a lively, noisy experience. I wonder now how the driver kept his sanity, especially while driving up and around those dangerous coastal curves. He must have had nerves of steel. I earned a large green *"G"* letter that season. Proud didn't begin to express my sentiment! I begged Aunt Ora and Uncle Kile, "Please come to just one of our games," but they never did. I participated with so much interest in many of the school's activities; I was especially fascinated with debating, particularly about notable politicians. Uncle Kile, who at one time had been a teacher, had great sport coaching me at home. He made it fun. What a thrill it was to come home shouting with excitement, "We won, Uncle Kile! You should have been there."

I received a part in the school play, which delighted and thrilled me, but it also gave me my first experience concerning stage fright. Singing in front of an audience was so commonplace and natural for me that it never occurred to me that acting would be so totally different. The night of the play I became paralyzed with stage fright, so frightened that I came close to forgetting my lines, but I managed to scrape through it without a mishap, which was a miracle. My good friend Doug was elected to see me home after the play since the folks would not be attending my performance. I was overjoyed to see him waiting for me! I needed a friend! "Well, you did okay. But you sure could have done better. Talk about stiff! You looked as though you had seen a ghost," he said with a disgusted tone.

"Doug, I was scared to death!" I shouted back.

"You should have taken a deep breath, relaxed, and walked like this," Doug said while mimicking a swinging girl's way of walking with one hand on his hip and the other hand outstretched as though he might wallop someone. Laugh? I couldn't help myself. My six-foot friend was such a special humorist. Because he never intended to be funny, he was indeed expressing his support.

"I have an idea. Let's walk to Barview and see if we can't beat the storm they say is coming," Doug suggested. I agreed, knowing well that I was to come straight home after the play. Tomorrow would be a hard day, as it was time again to drive out to the Salem dentist to have my braces tightened once again. *Well,* I thought, *the folks don't know when the play is over, so why not?* I assumed there was ample time. All day long there had been talk of a storm on the way. It was so balmy and quiet. What a perfect time for a walk since we both were dressed for the rain, rubber boots included. *Why not!* we thought, so we both strutted like two peacocks over and down to the railroad tracks.

On our merry way to Barview, we were two lighthearted, impulsive teenagers about as giddy as they come! Of course, Doug had to show off his masculine gender by telling a few spooky stories, hoping, of course, that I would lose my poise and become in a skittish twitter. "Doug, you don't scare me!" I said, when quite suddenly the sky became extremely black. It was as though God had pulled a black curtain around us. The once soft breeze was becoming stronger and stronger. The once peaceful silence was broken by the surf's breakers hitting the jetty rocks with a cracking, crashing sound. I placed my hands in front of my face and not even an outline of my hands could be seen. Neither one of us hesitated to turn back. Believe me, we left in full steam! Not one word was spoken by either one of us. The wind was now so forceful I could barely walk against it and since it was so black around us, I couldn't see Doug next to me. I hung on to him for dear life, desperately attempting to keep up with him, my two steps to his one. By the time we reached Garibaldi the waves were spraying water up on the tracks and the rain had drenched us. My legs were in agony from my wet boots rubbing my skin with every step I took. It felt like knives scraping into my flesh. It was a very painful endeavor walking up our hill to my very dark house while noticing Doug's house was lit up like a Christmas tree. I thought I would sneak into our enclosed back porch and take off my soaked coat and headgear. What a relief to pull out of my miserable boots, then I very quietly and with much caution opened the back door, ready to tiptoe up to my room. But I became more than dismayed to see Uncle Kile standing in front of me with his arm raised and positioned to strike me! In fright, I ran under his arm and into my room before he could land a blow! Nothing much was ever said again, but poor Doug was grounded for a month! It was still raining lightly the next morning and there was debris everywhere from the night's storm. "And to think you were out in this!" Aunt Ora said. She saw my blistered legs but she said nothing. I am sure she felt that I deserved the punishment, and even more.

The night's howling rainstorm and now the high tides caused the already swollen rivers to gush over their banks, causing flooding everywhere. It was especially bad for us driving through the high water into Tillamook. I will never, as long as I live, forget the salmon flipping and flopping in the swift water in front of and to the side of our car as we drove through the water, the unbelievable sight of seeing salmon struggling as they pitifully were tangled in the barbed wire fences. Not a word was said because of the stressful duress we were feeling. As we drove further away from the coast everything around us appeared as though we had just come out from behind a cloud. It was wonderful to see the cheerful sun. "I'll tell you, Nadine! I hope your teeth are worth all of this turmoil," Aunt Ora announced.

I was invited to a Halloween party that year, which I thought was more than just special. It was just for upperclassmen, so this made me feel quite exceptional. Finally I would get to see what dunking for apples and other games were all about. Since it wasn't a costume party, Aunt Ora decided I should have a new dress for the occasion. Of course, this pleased me. After all, I wanted to be in a party fashion, not wearing everyday school clothes.

It was a party all right. There were no parents around and I didn't see anything that resembled dunking for apples. There were a few games such as spinning the bottle and post office. I was wishing that I had paid attention to several of my friends: "You really shouldn't go to that party," but I knew more than they did. *Well, here I am,* I thought. I was trying desperately not to appear mortified and childish, as I am sure I did, in spite of my efforts. Boys were kissing girls. Girls were hugging and kissing boys. I ended up by kicking shins and stepping on toes. Two boys got me behind a curtain. I escaped them by kicking and then going for my coat. One of the boys offered to take me home. I thought this would be all right. After all, he was a son of a minister. He tried to put his arm around me, but I moved out of his reach. I once again came home to a dark house. Aunt Ora's only question the next day was, "Did you have fun?" Not "Who was there," nothing at all about the party.

"No, it really wasn't fun. Not one doughnut. There wasn't even any apple cider," I told her.

My most beautiful memory of this year was our spring band concert. Our high school was at the top of the hill which had a view of all views of the Tillamook Bay. This was our setting for the concert. It was a gorgeous, warm spring evening. We were all so thrilled and bubbling over with enthusiasm. It was pleasing also to see many parents and friends attending. Even though I didn't have parents, I had friends. It made our year's work seem worthwhile and our concert more important. I was to sing a solo with the band towards the end of the concert, which was the popular song *The Isle of Capri.* Neil was so afraid that I wouldn't allow myself enough time to put my saxophone in place and be in front of the band on cue, he invariably would kick me in the shins and take my saxophone from me. Tonight was no different. I was kicked! If anyone noticed, it was ignored. The sky was so bright with the most brilliant red and orange sunset colors ever. It was breathtaking in the manner it reflected over the smooth, deep blue water of the bay. I was filled with emotional enjoyment. How I loved to sing! I thought, *I do have so much to sing about.*

The applause was a heartwarming experience. The praise and hugs I experienced was overwhelming. Neil's smile was worth a million dollars. I had made it. Mr. Dunn, our band leader, was looking for my aunt. I told him with embarrassment, "Oh, she didn't come because she was too tired."

He patted me on the shoulder and said, "Too bad that she missed your solo. We all were so proud of you."

Mr. and Mrs. Garrison were there and she said with a scowl, "You did just fine." Then she added, "Come see me one day soon." I wondered why on earth she couldn't smile. Mr. Garrison knew how when he said with a broad smile, "That was great. You did us proud." Wow, that made me feel good!

I did go over to Mrs. Garrison's house the next day because of my curiosity as to why she wanted to visit with me, of all people. I disliked going to her house for fear I might disturb or tarnish something. As I sat there in one of her straight, stiff chairs, a feeling of cold contempt slowly but surely was developing inside me. As I stared into her stony white face and eyes of blue steel, I knew well that I was in for some sort of lecture. She didn't let me down! "You have too many boys around you all of the time. How about that Halloween party? I heard plenty about that. Boys are never up to any good! Not when girls are around." She continued on and on. "Even that school band is nearly all boys."

I couldn't take any more without losing my temper, so I excused myself politely. As I was attempting to leave, she abruptly handed me a stack of *True Story* magazines. "Now, you read these, young lady. You will learn that I am right." She used harsh, severe words as I continued to walk away from her.

They were considered trashy magazines for those times, but being a typical kid, I was intrigued and fascinated. Wow! Sizzle, sizzle! Mrs. Garrison, you were a wild woman! What an education she gave me.

I knew my Uncle Chet and his lawyers had taken our custody case on up to Supreme Court, but I was not the least bit concerned because I was so positive that he would lose. I couldn't have been more mistaken! He won the guardianship along with being administrator for Sylvia and me. We were to be at the Tillamook Courthouse on the first Monday of our summer vacation with all of our belongings. We had only two days to prepare for our move. I felt as though I had just awakened from a bad dream. "It isn't true! It isn't true!" I kept repeating.

"Oh, but it is!" Aunt Ora said. She was so angry and continued to stay angry as we gathered and packed our belongings. We searched for the nicest box that we could find to carry Sugarpie in. After all, she was our most important treasure.

Aunt Ora and Mrs. Garrison repeatedly told us to "Make your Uncle Chet and Aunt Florence so miserable that they would gladly send you back here. He hates cats in the house, you know!" (Another worry for us! A worry that we didn't need!)

I managed not to cry until it came time to say good-bye to our friends. Then we all cried. I had never before seen little Sylvia so heartbroken. She loved it there as much as I did, so the two of us decided to console ourselves by taking our last Sunday walk down the tracks for the last time. It was a beautiful June Sunday, but our hearts were so full of grief that weather truly didn't matter. After all, our home was being taken away from us, along with our friends. And I was so frightened of being locked up in this girls' school that I had been hearing so much about. "It will be the same as a prison," Aunt Ora had said so many times.

Yes, this was a worrisome walk we were taking until we spotted Mr. Garrison coming towards us, waving. "You girls wait up," he called to us. I was so happy to see him! We did need a friend and I could tell that he wanted to talk to us. Thank God he did! "I want you girls to under-stand that your Uncle Chester is not a bad man. He loves you very much. He wouldn't have gone through so much if he didn't want to take care of you two." Then he begged us not to deliberately cause trouble like Lizzy (Mrs. Garrison) and Aunt Ora were telling us to do. "You will be making yourselves so miserable. Your uncle and Aunt Florence will be giving you both such a wonderful home, so you both shouldn't be so sad. I'm sure you can come back for a visit. I'm saying these things to you, because I don't like seeing you girls so unhappy." I did feel better after Mr. Garrison's words of wisdom, but Sylvia was still heartsick and, in her own mind, fighting the move. I had so much respect for Mr. Garrison so I was sure he knew what he was telling us. I remembered also that he was a retired lawyer. He walked along with us for some time, then excused himself by saying, "Come see us, now, when you visit Garibaldi." I prom-ised him that we would.

All of this was a mystery to me. Why should it be happening? And I am sure that for Sylvia it was more than she could comprehend. We walked in silence for some time, then I asked her, "Do you think, Sylvia, that Uncle Chet and Aunt Florence want us this much? They have sure gone to a lot of trouble."

"Maybe they do, but I don't want to go," she said with a tone filled with defiance. We were going to say good-bye to my old friend, the lake, but I decided that I couldn't do it. Anyway, *I'll be back*, I promised myself.

Chapter Thirteen

Monday morning was almost one of complete silence as Uncle Kile was packing the car full of our belongings, angry Sugarpie included. As we were ready to leave, neighbors and friends were there with good-byes. Yes, there were tears, especially from Aunt Ora. Uncle Kile had turned ashen white as we drove away to Tillamook.

Uncle Chet and his lawyer were parked in front of the court-house, waiting for our arrival. No one spoke as Uncle Chet and Uncle Kile transferred our belongings to the other car. Uncle Chet carefully placed Sugarpie in the back seat next to us. Believe me, we both watched her move with wide eyes. I was tickled inside that he showed gentleness. *At least we are starting out on the right foot!* I was thinking.

Uncle Chet and his attorney were having a great time visiting and chuckling as we were leaving Tillamook. I couldn't understand what could possibly be so funny. When we were about halfway through the trip, Sylvia began crying. She had become frightened because of the speed Uncle Chet was driving, so much faster that we were accustomed to. I attempted to console her, but my efforts were useless. Finally, I tapped Uncle Chet on the shoulder and said to him, "Uncle Chet, I really think that Sylvia would stop crying if you would promise to get her a new bicycle. She loves blue. I would like to have a bicycle too, but I don't really care what color it is. I wish, too, that you wouldn't go so fast. Sylvia is scared and crying. Sugarpie might feel better too." She was fiercely, frantically trying to escape from her box. He did slow down, but he didn't say a word about the bicycles except only, "We will see."

Mr. Creason, the lawyer, was about to split his sides from a case of old fashioned snickers. I realize today that Mr. Creason could see the big changes developing in his friend's life style. It would never be the same. But at that time I thought of him as a very silly man! Sylvia stopped crying. I think she was visualizing a bright new bicycle. Sugarpie was grumbling and growling as much as ever. I couldn't help myself—I was becoming excited as we approached Dallas. When Uncle Chet parked in front of his beautiful, spacious house, I became anxious and a little apprehensive as, with Sylvia behind me, we went up the front steps and into the house. I couldn't greet Aunt Florence fast enough. And what a reunion it was!

There were many beautiful, happy events this day, especially to see Sugarpie adapt so perfectly. Of course, she was beside herself just to be out of her box. "How dare you!" she was telling us as she ruffled her fur coat. She remembered Dallas since she had lived next door at one time. As far as Uncle Chet was concerned, well, he acted as though he didn't notice her, as she was becoming quite comfortable in his house. He gave himself away, however, by bringing home the best cat food that he could buy. This was one of our biggest worries. What would Uncle Chet do about Sugarpie? Yes, we were like two little old ladies when it came to our Sugarpie's welfare.

Our gorgeous pink and white feminine room was so beautiful it somehow didn't seem real. Aunt Florence must have spent weeks planning the décor. It was a large room. At one end was a sitting and study area which was furnished with Mother and Dad's living room furniture, and at the other end was our bedroom. The window treatments were lovely white crisscross Priscillas, every young girl's dream. "Sylvia, I think I could stay up here forever," I said. "

I could too," she said. We both were ecstatic to each have our own walk-in closets.

"Oh, I don't believe it," I said while dancing around the room.

I noticed Sylvia was repeatedly looking out of the window. "It seems funny doesn't it, to not see the old bay and all of the big green trees?" We both had enjoyed them so much and also watching the small fishing boats from our Garibaldi window, especially at sunset.

"Well, Sylvia, you know we still have a nice view. We can see the old courthouse clock, which is up there in the tower. It looks like a full moon at night, but really better than a moon, because we will always know what time it is. Even in the middle of the night it will shine right into our room." It was amazing how I satisfied myself as well as my little sister.

We spent most of this first day becoming familiar with our new home and I rather imagine we made Aunt Florence somewhat dizzy from all of our chatter and questions, one right after another. She couldn't help but see the glow of blissfulness from both of us, as we were bubbling over with happy exuberance. This must have been a sensational reward for her. She had no idea as to what to expect from us.

One of my many questions for Aunt Florence was about a beautiful tiny rocker that was in the living room. It looked as though it was Grandma's but never was hers as eye-appealing as this chair. "That was your grandmother's little chair. And since it is such a valuable antique, I decided to restore it," was her explanation.

"Wouldn't Grandma be thrilled?" I said to her. I couldn't believe how beautiful it had become. The mahogany frame was refinished into a very soft luster and her blue needlepoint with shades of pink and rose flowers were indeed exquisite. Only Aunt Florence would have thought of creating this ugly little chair into such a thing of beauty. And how brilliant she was to have done this!

The coming evening we had another lovely surprise. Aunt Florence had invited several of our Dallas classmates to dinner. The gathering was somewhat uncomfortable for me at first, as I felt tense and quite shy. Never before had we experienced our very own dinner party and it had been so long since I had seen or heard from any of my old pals. I felt as though I were a stranger. But before long we were chattering like jaybirds. I was interested to hear about many of my friends and newsy tidbits. I was curious regarding my teachers and, oh yes, the school band! They enjoyed hearing about some of my adventures and about living over on the coast. Sylvia and her friends were having a marvelous time also. Aunt Florence was clever by inviting Pat Tracy, a friend of mine. "Oh, haven't you heard, Nadine? I'm going to St. Helen's Hall this year," she said.

My heart jumped and I said, "Why, Pat? Why would you want to go to that awful place?"

"It isn't an awful place." She then went on and on as to how wonderful it was.

Helen Hamilton kept saying, "I sure wish I could go there." I wanted to tell her that she could go in my place, but I didn't. Thank heavens the subject was changed and we continued to have a typical teen-age good time.

What a day this one had been! A day filled with so many emotional highs and lows. We both were tired and I was wondering what tomorrow might bring. Sylvia was so cute when she glanced outside from our bedroom window. Excitedly she said, "Nadine! The moon is saying that it is eleven o'clock! We better hurry up and go to sleep."

The next morning I decided to satisfy some of my curiosities by quietly asking about Herman without appearing to be intrusive. I was delighted and surprised to learn that Aunt Florence and Uncle Chet had been taking care of Herman prior to Grandma's passing away. Every summer they had him home for a vacation and the next week he would be with us for a week. *How very wonderful,* I was thinking. "We will be so happy to help with Herman," I said.

Aunt Florence laughed when she said, "I remember how you girls helped before. Yes, I'm sure we will need you."

I also learned this morning that a trip to Alaska was planned; Alaska, so far away, a place I had never imagined or thought about. I should have been excited, but I could not comprehend such a trip. My attention was focused more upon Herman's visit. "You girls haven't looked out back yet this morning, have you?" Aunt Florence asked. When we did glance out back, I was stunned beyond belief! There sat two shiny bicycles! One was blue, the other a gorgeous green. We both were so overcome that neither one of us could speak. Of course, Sylvia knew immediately the blue one was hers and I was absolutely wild with my very own dark, lucent, green bike. Down deep inside of me I was inclined to be unassertive and timid toward my seemingly austere uncle, but when he stood beside those two bikes that morning, his eyes twinkled brighter than any star. He wanted to laugh, but he didn't dare! Heaven forbid, no one should know how much he loved these two girls. And me! I did forget my negative self-consciousness completely. "Thank you! Those are the most beautiful bicycles in the world!" I didn't hug him, but I remember touching and giving his hand a squeeze. I would have never wanted to embarrass him.

Finally the day arrived. Herman was home! Sylvia and I were the first to greet him. He looked just the same, as I remembered. "Remember me, Herman?" I asked.

"Your name is Maydene, and you are Susie Ann. Ha, ha, Maydene." He thought he had really fooled me. He carefully placed his brown felt hat upon the hall tree and took his suitcase up to his room. It was amazing how neat and tidy he was. The next thing was to locate his favorite rocker and he didn't waste any time getting his chair into motion. The more he rocked the faster he talked. The two seemed to go together. "A rock'in and a talk'n!"

"Who are you talking to, Herman?" we would ask him.

"Oh now, Maydene," he would say. Aunt Florence would watch his chair nervously. Finally, she asked us to please place a small rug under his rocker. She feared soon his chair would wear bald marks into the carpet.

Herman thought he was a musician so nothing else would do— Herman had to have his own violin. He sawed the violin while he rocked. Sylvia and I took turns as his accompanist. He adored *Red Wing* so *Red Wing* it was. People who walked by the house must have thought we all had gone mad! Of course, Sylvia and I were just about hysterical with laughter. Aunt Florence must have had nerves of steel. Her sense of humor saved her day, I am sure. It would tickle the life out of us when I would sing a song for Herman, which he loved. When I would come to a high note, he would join in and shout, "Boop-boop!" as if he were trying to boost me up there. "Let's dance and see what Herman does!" we decided, so we had what sounded much like a hoe-down. Herman joined in with his violin. Yes, we indeed were reprehended!

Our first dinner with Herman was one to remember. Uncle Chet proudly brought salmon steaks home for the occasion, and when Herman refused to eat his, Uncle Chet became quite irritated, to say the least. "Herman, eat your salmon!" he ordered.

"No, Chester, it has bones in it," he said very emphatically.

"Damnit, Herman, you eat that salmon." Uncle Chet was

determined. I cringed, as I was in sympathy with Herman. I hated those tiny, fine, annoying bones myself. So what happened? Herman got a bone stuck in his throat. It was a wild dinner all right, but Herman survived and the dinner ended on a happy note, thanks to Aunt Florence!

"How about an after-dinner smoke, Herman?" Uncle Chet asked with a twinkle in his eye.

"Ah now, Chester," Herman said, feeling embarrassed and backward. "Florence's house will get smelled up." But nothing would do. Uncle Chet insisted by holding a package of Chesterfields in front of Herman and he eventually took a cigarette while smiling from ear to ear. He held the cigarette with his thumb and index finger as Uncle Chet lit it. Herman didn't draw in on the cigarette, instead he blew through it. Smoke and sparks flew. He resembled a giant sparkler! I tried hard not to laugh, but the more he puffed away, the funnier it became. Sparks were flying and we all were in hysterics. Herman snickered and sputtered, joining in with the fun. Uncle Chet, well, he chuckled under his breath.

The next morning was to be Herman's annual shopping day with Uncle Chet. Just as soon as the stores opened, they would be on their way. Uncle Chet was always dressed to a "T," nothing ever out of place. Herman tried to be as spiffy. He walked beside his brother with a light bounce to his step all decked out in his brown suit, bright tie, and wearing his faithful brown felt hat. Even a stranger could see how proud and full of joy this dear person was feeling.

Several hours had passed since the two had left for their shopping spree. "What in the world has happened to those two? They have been gone for hours." Aunt Florence was becoming anxious.

Another hour had passed since they had gone when I decided to glance down the front walk. "They are coming now. Wow! Of all of the packages!" I declared. But I knew immediately Uncle Chet was annoyed. He was several steps ahead of Herman, even though Herman was jogging right along.

My thought was to stay clear, especially when Aunt Florence questioned Chet. "What in the world took you so long?"

"Hell, you can take him next time," was his answer. I learned later that Uncle Chet wanted Herman to try on a gray or a blue suit and Herman refused. He would only look at brown suits. "We had a hell of a time trying to get the pants on and off over those new tennis shoes. I should have gotten his new shoes last because he wouldn't take them off once the clerk had put them on him. I couldn't get him to try on a new hat. He won't part with the old one. Everyone in the store was trying to get him to at least try on a new one. He wouldn't budge. 'I'll only wear my brown hat!' Herman stubbornly repeated while hugging his old hat, so let him wear the damn hat till it rots."

"Oh now, Chester, as long as he is happy that is what matters."

Aunt Florence was trying to smooth over what had been an irritating experience.

"Well, how are you going to get those tennis shoes off of him tonight?" Uncle Chet asked her with a grin.

"Herman wouldn't do that, I'm sure. He knows better, I'm sure." She was only trying to convince herself, so we all went about our own way, doing our own thing for the rest of the day, forgetting about Herman and his treasured tennis shoes.

When bedtime came, Aunt Florence reminded Herman to be sure and take off his tennis shoes. "Oh now, Florence" Herman answered, which meant that he had no intentions of taking off his shoes.

"Herman, you'll get the bed sheets dirty. Not only that, but isn't good for your feet," Aunt Florence pleaded with him while Uncle Chet sat behind his newspaper with that all-knowing expression "I told you so." Our very refined, proper aunt was horrified. "The idea, Herman. I am ashamed!" she said to him.

"Oh now, Florence" Herman said, as he belligerently marched to his room.

"Girls, can't you persuade him?" Aunt Florence asked.

I wondered and thought about it for quite awhile, then I said. "Okay, we will give it try." Up the stairs we went and then proceeded to knock softly on his door. "Herman, why won't you take your tennis shoes off? You know, Aunt Florence is going to cry if you don't."

"That's right, Herman. She will cry if you don't get those shoes off," Sylvia said.

There were several minutes of silence, then we heard two thuds hit the floor. Herman called to us, "Don't you steal my shoes." That was one of the reasons he wished to keep his shoes on. We were all sorry, as he must have experienced thievery at sometime. We assured him that his shoes were safe with us.

The next few days were pleasant ones with Herman. We had such fun teaching and coaching him to say the days of the week. I don't know who was more proud, Herman, Sylvia, or me, of the accomplishment. In the meantime we had promised to take him up town to the band concert, which was Saturday night. So now when he said the days of the week, instead of just saying Saturday, in an explosive, excited manner he would shout, "Saturday night!" We couldn't believe our ears, including several of my girlfriends who thought so fondly of Herman. We all went together to the Saturday night band concert with Herman wearing his tennis shoes, new brown suit, and the old brown felt hat—and a smile which no one could destroy. His ears were filled with music and his appetite was satisfied with one bag after another of popcorn. Which one of us had the most fun? I'm not at all sure!

Herman was to go back to the state institution that Sunday. I was feeling sad and concerned for him. This was wasted, negative energy on my part, because he was like most all children, excited and eager to return home. He became so engrossed with gathering up and packing his things, he literally hummed. I have never seen anyone who could be so immersed in their own feverish activity as Herman. Every minute was priceless. He didn't have one spare minute for conversing with himself, which was his favorite thing to do. "Well, I guess I better get Herman and his gear to the car so we get him back to the school on time," Uncle Chet said as he called for Herman. There was no answer from him, so we all began searching for Herman from room to room.

"What in the world has happened to him?" Aunt Florence wondered. We even looked down in the basement and all around the outside of the house.

"I'll be damned! He's in the car," Uncle Chet said. There he was sitting in the car, anxiously waiting with his old brown felt hat on his head and staring straight ahead, with not one good-bye! He was ready to go home!

Aunt Florence was weary after Herman had gone back to his home. Even though we had a wonderful housekeeper to clean and cook, it was the commotion which was stressful for her. "I was scared, Nadine, that you would drag out that saxophone," she said.

"I did think about it but was afraid that I would scare Herman."

"Herman might have taken for the hills, all right. I'm sure I would have had a heart attack." We had a good laugh.

Aunt Florence's health problems (paralysis) had not improved. The truth was, it was worsening and it had become more of a struggle for her to walk. The toe of her right foot would drag and she would also lose her balance, especially when she became overly tired. But never did she complain. Instead, she would say, "Oh, I am so fortunate not to be in pain. And I thank God every day that I have my own mind." Her handicap never in a million years ruined her zest for life. I loved her sense of humor, it was fabulous. And if she wanted to go somewhere, she went! But one of her most valuable qualities was her appreciation of all that was beautiful. If she couldn't see the beauty in it, she would then beautify it. Since the house had become somewhat quieter and at peace again with Herman gone, she decided to busy herself back in her favorite, gentle, unreserved sewing room with Sugarpie by her side. When I saw what she was doing. I became fascinated. I wanted to be with her in this cheerful little room. She had an old black and white photograph which she had decided to touch up with her oil paints and trusty paintbrush. "This old picture should be out in the open so we all can enjoy it. Now, don't you think it is pretty? It just needed a little help," she said.

"It is beautiful, Aunt Florence." I was amazed, as it seemed like magic to me.

"Now that I have you to myself, Nadine. I want to talk to you and tell you how much your uncle and I appreciate you girls. And it is so wonderful for us having you. But you know, I really think you should write to your Aunt Ora. She must wonder how you are. Once a week you should write."

"Okay, Aunt Florence," I agreed. She didn't know that I had already begun a letter. "I like writing letters. And I have wondered in the back of my mind if they were all right," I said.

"Now there is another matter that I feel we should discuss. Though I hate to bring it up," she said.

I knew what it was. I had been expecting it, so I said, "It is about Uncle Frank, isn't it?" as I reached down for Sugarpie. I yearned to feel her cushy, warm body next to me as this torturous incident was about to be discussed. I could feel my body stiffen and my words were blunt and cold with hurt as I repeated the entire ugly story to her, the same story I told before to my father. It was just as vivid this day as it was then. And just as sickening, embarrassing, and as frightening. I could feel myself tremble, even while holding Sugarpie so close to me. "I don't understand why Aunt Ada could be so uncaring," I said. "She just didn't care at all. That was the worst part." Then I began to lose control of my tears. "When they come here to see you and Uncle Chet, can't Sylvia and I go somewhere?" I asked.

Aunt Florence had tears of hurt also when she said, "I am so sorry, Nadine, that I had to put you through this. But we had to know. Your poor father tried to tell us, but he was so beside himself he couldn't. We only knew part of what happened. Now then, they will be out here the day of the Henkle reunion. You and Sylvia can spend the day with friends, or you can be with us. I don't expect you to ever forget or even under-stand what happened, but you must realize that this awful thing your Uncle Frank did to you was an act of sickness. Just that, sick. Forgiving him will take time. Running away from all of this will never bring forgive-ness. Not being able to forgive will hurt you more than it will your Uncle Frank. But no, you will never forget. I must tell you, too, that your Aunt Ada has always been crazy about you two girls. Did you know that she even wanted you for her own? So maybe she has been hurt more than anyone else. No, we just can't understand everything. But thank our good Father above. We can forgive." Aunt Florence, and her precious words!

"One thing I do know, Nadine. Frank will never hurt you again. No, not as long as your Uncle Chet is around. But I do want you to remem-ber one thing, Ada is his sister, the same as Sylvia is yours, and we all want to be together in harmony," she said.

"Will Uncle Roy be here for the reunion?" I asked.

"Yes, he surely will," she said. Then she asked, "Does this mean you might go to the reunion?"

I could only say, "Maybe." Down deep, I wanted to go. I wanted to belong! Aunt Florence knew this as we both left that delightful little sewing room with Sugarpie stretching herself as if she had just spent the most comfy afternoon of her life.

It was amazing for me to realize that just a few months ago I had felt nothing more than being a bother to everyone. Now there we were in the care of two people who radiated their love around and about us. How they did want us to have the best of everything. I felt so special and important when they would insist upon knowing where we were at all times. They appreciated my not being rebellious and becoming resentful. They didn't realize that I cared so much that they cared. Of course, there were times I would forget to tell Aunt Florence where I was going because in Garibaldi no one really expressed concerns. This was a new experience and I liked it. Many times I would think about Mr. Garrison and what he had had to say to Sylvia and me, "Give your Aunt and Uncle a chance." How I wish I could say thank you for that valuable advice. I had not once invited the whale!

Aunt Florence had a fabulous eye for fashion and definitely a passion for pretty clothes. She was more than just a little anxious to take us wardrobe shopping in Salem. I say we three drove because while Aunt Florence did the steering, Sylvia and I took turns maneuvering her lame foot on the gas peddle and brake. Our system was one of a kind. It was hilarious then, but would have been a disaster in today's traffic. Our shopping was fun and also a bit overwhelming. What lovely dresses we came home with. "Whatever you do, girls, don't tell your uncle about our driving scheme!" she cautioned.

On the day of the Henkle reunion I decided to go, even though I felt nervous and quivery inside because of the thought of being in the same room with Uncle Frank and Aunt Ada. Aunt Florence kept her promise by staying close to me at all times. How very uncomfortable it must have been for those two people.

The reunion was held at my birthplace, Philomath, where over a hundred Henkles meet every year. They traveled to the Willamette Valley from all over the United States. The dinner always was a potluck. With so much food, one thought they would never eat again. After the meal there was a program followed by boring, boring speech after speech. Thank heavens Aunt Florence excused Sylvia and me. We joined other kids, and I remember thinking *What odd kids,* as there wasn't much to talk about, let alone do!

I am glad I took that first courageous step of exposing myself to these two people. Aunt Ada and I exchanged smiles, but I didn't have the spunk to look in Uncle Frank's direction. Was it fear, embarrassment, or guilt? I didn't know. What a pleasure seeing Uncle Roy again. When he came to me and said, "You stick with your Aunt Florence, and everything will go good for you two girls," I remembered those last words from my dad: "If you have any problem, go to your Uncle Roy." So Uncle Roy could have never known how much I treasured his valuable advice.

We were all glad when the reunion came to an end and we were back home where we could relax. Aunt Florence complimented Sylvia and me. "I was so proud of you two girls. You looked so nice in your new dresses. You both were such ladies."

"We didn't know anyone, so there wasn't anything else to do but be ladies," I wanted to say. I was glad Aunt Florence went back into her sewing room. "Aunt Florence, I wonder, could it have been my fault that Uncle Frank did those things to me?"

"My heavens, no! It wasn't your fault. What makes you even think such a thing?" She was stunned.

"I couldn't look at him today," I said. "Maybe I did something wrong that made him do those things."

"Now, you listen to me! You didn't do anything wrong! There are some men who can't leave little girls alone. This is the sickness I have been talking about. We had a neighbor who did this to a little friend of mine. It wasn't her fault either. You have no reason to ever feel guilty. Instead, I am awfully proud of you. You know, I think the best thing for you to do is to think of nothing else but the exciting, happy events that are coming into your life. You will be surprised how the unfavorable times will fade away."

The next few weeks were the busiest and most exciting weeks of my young life. Yes, we were really going to Alaska, so there was much planning and shopping to do for this incredible trip. Time was going so fast that we barely had enough time left for summer swimming and enjoying those new bicycles.

Uncle Chet and Aunt Florence's friends, the Congers, and Aunt Florence's widowed sister, Ivy, were taking the Alaskan trip with us. Before I knew it we were all in Seattle together, just in time to celebrate Sylvia's eleventh birthday, which was held in a very elaborate restaurant. She was presented with a gorgeous cake with all of the trimmings. I couldn't have been more excited or thrilled if it had been my birthday. It was as though we all were in a movie. I felt as ritzy and foxy as a famous Hollywood star. This was a night of all nights.

The next day we were on board a beautiful cruise ship and we truly were on our way to Alaska. I was overflowing with disbelief. It didn't seem real to me, two girls who had never gone any further than a few miles in Oregon. Naturally we were intrigued with the ship, especially by our state room, the beautifully prepared meals, and the constant attention from the ship's handsome officers. I thought to myself how lucky I was to finally get those braces off of my teeth, so I didn't hesitate giving a smile whenever one of the officers looked in my direction. We were in a completely new world and we were enjoying every minute of it. Sylvia and I both thought the dinner gong was the prettiest tune we had ever heard. I never failed to write letters and cards every day to Aunt Ora and Uncle Kile.

The most beautiful remembrance of the trip for me was the Columbia Glacier. I could never find words to express its beauty and the thrill of seeing Mount McKinley. The husky sled dogs will never be forgotten. One very bad experience for me was my seasick episode. It is true that if a person is seasick enough, they really don't care if they live or die. That was me! I was the only one in our group to get seasick, so of course there was teasing. Uncle Chet kept telling me, "It all is in your head." But he became quite sick while going up and around those narrow curves while traveling by train in the interior of Alaska. I didn't have to say a word, he knew what I was thinking.

The Congers and Ivy were good sports and great travelers, so there was harmony throughout the trip. Hemerly Conger was more fun that a barrel of monkeys. Now, he had one very important passion on this trip. That was to see at least one moose in the wilds. We ended up by taking him to the museum in Juneau. At least he got to see a stuffed one. Yes, the trip was filled with many delightful memories, partly because Sylvia and I could see the humor in most everything, especially with and about dear Ivy. She was so proper and such a perfect lady, but when shocked or startled she would literally become unglued. She would squeal, be highly insulted, or embarrassed.

Now, up at Mount McKinely we had what I call tent-like cabins to spend the night in. One very bad feature was the large mosquitoes. I have never seen anything bring as much misery as they did, but we were equally fascinated by the adorable little chipmunks that were scampering and hustling everywhere. When Sylvia and I noticed how the little rascals were invading Ivy's cabin, we deliberately shut her tent door. When she returned, she was horrified to see chipmunks jumping and running everywhere. They were having the time of their lives, even in her luggage. She flew from her cabin squealing and leaping as though she had been confronted by a million beasts. She almost lost her hat along with her composure! We all had a good laugh. No one dreamed that we had shut her door, except Hemerly. His face turned red as he chuckled, sputtered, and nearly swallowed a mouthful of tobacco!

Hemerly and Uncle Chet became brave souls and flew from Fairbanks to Nome in a biplane. In those days that was really a daring thing to do. We all were relieved to have them safely back with their feet on the ground. When we asked them as to how the trip was, Uncle Chet said proudly, "Well, we shook hands with Jesus Christ himself!" No one thought it was very funny except Sylvia and me.

Since the Presbyterian minister from Dallas was now serving the church in Fairbanks, Aunt Florence was filled with enthusiastic interest to see and visit with him. Naturally, he and his wife were excited to have someone from their hometown, especially Aunt Florence, call upon them. Nothing would do but "Please share dinner with us." We accepted their invitation. Needless to say, Aunt Florence was pleased, but Hemerly and Uncle Chet had to have a few nips beforehand to muster up their courage, which made the evening a little tense for Aunt Florence, but interesting. I held my breath every time Uncle Chet mentioned Nome. When he offered to give the blessing, I thought Ivy was going to go into shock for sure. We all survived the evening but were relieved when it was over. Ivy sighed, "Oh dear, oh dear," all of the way back to the hotel.

When it was time to board the cruise ship for home, I was given seasick medication which made the return trip wonderful to me. Even when Sylvia chewed on caramels, it didn't upset me. The Gulf of Alaska was a delightful pleasure. The last night of the voyage, a very elaborate, formal dinner party was given with music and dancing. *Just like in the movies,* I thought. To my amazement Hemerly and Uncle Chet were the most popular guests there. They were both dressed up like clowns with seasick cartoons pinned to the front of their costumes. No one would have dreamed that this was my dignified, serious uncle, so I am more than happy to have this very dear memory of him. Sylvia and I were dressed in our very best evening dresses. My dress was my first formal gown of pink taffeta. I felt like a princess. Even though I had never danced before, I did this night with my uncle, my first partner. I can still hear his words of instructions. "One, two, slide. Step along now." I was having the time of my life. The facial expression of Aunt Florence was one of angelic endearment. Her eyes sparkled with sweet love as she watched us. She must have been thanking God.

I continued to write to Aunt Ora and Uncle Kile and sent carefully chosen picture cards from Alaska, but still received not a line from them. Then, lo and behold, came a letter from Mrs. Garrison. It frightened me at first, thinking that something had happened to Aunt Ora, but no, the letter was ugly and bitter, accusing me of deliberately hurting Aunt Ora by bragging about our fancy new home and our expensive activities. I was crushed and stunned by her words. How could they think of me this way? I finally gave the letter to Aunt Florence, as her curiosity was quite obvious. She was shocked and disgusted with Mrs. Garrison's revolting, accusative words because none of it was true. "I think your Uncle Chet is right, Nadine. He has always said that she was the culprit behind your Aunt Ora. Why, I don't know," she said. "But if I were you, I would continue to write. Not as often perhaps, but enough to show her that you do care for her and that you are above those shallow falsehoods. You know, I wouldn't even mention Mrs. Garrison." What a wonderful lesson this was. One of my lifelong treasures.

How fast this summer was going, so there weren't many days left for swimming down at the park or for other fun summer things to do. And, too, we had to think and plan about going away to school, which still was very scary for me. Time wasn't standing still. It was getting closer, closer! The folks felt it would be wise if we visited the school so that we would have some idea about it before we jumped in. It was better than sight unseen, so for the first time I saw the stately, ivy-covered brick building which was surrounded by an immaculate lawn and garden. Sylvia and I met all five of the Episcopal sisters and we liked them all very much, so this part was a relief for us. Sister Margaret Helena visited with us in the parlor, which was a beautiful big room filled with heavy, ornate furniture. I was overcome with the beauty of the massive antique grand piano. It was gorgeous, as was the thick, peacock blue oriental carpet. Wouldn't it be marvelous to sing a solo in this splendid room? This was a secret thought of mine as I admired that impressive, lavish piano.

There was much to do in preparing ourselves for boarding school, so many chores for Aunt Florence. The first and most important was buying our uniforms, which were navy, or brown, skirts with matching sweaters, and white cotton blouses. There were red ties to go with blue, or tan ties for the brown uniforms. Not bad looking at all. Our shoes and hose also were traditional. At night we were to either wear a white silk or a powder blue shirtwaist dress for dinner. It was wise to have both. Everything we owned had to have a name tag.

Since our Aunt Florence was a true perfectionist, every name tag was done with excellence and virtue. Nothing was packed that did not contain a name tape, including our umbrellas. She even handmade tiny satin envelopes to be pinned inside of our bras for spending money. I was shocked. "You can't be too careful in the big city," she said. The sisters insisted, too, that our tennis rackets be marked, which didn't set well with Aunt Florence because she couldn't mark them to suit her liking. Of all the struggling she went through without one grumble, I would have thrown them out of the window. On weekends we were not required to wear uniforms, so there was what I called a normal wardrobe to be marked and packed; also, evening coats and formal dresses since our school exchanged dances and parties with Hill Military School, which struck terror through my heart. Dancing with a boy! The thought of it paralyzed me. I desperately tried not to think about it. *The time will come fast enough without dwelling on it,* I would think.

Uncle Chet did not have the temperament to be at all interested in all of our hub-bub and trials regarding the big move for school. "What are you doing? Packing up the town of Dallas?" he would say. We ignored him so that he would move along and tend to his own business. We could then continue with ours. Paul would drop by at least once a day. I am sure he was hearing all kinds of comments from Uncle Chet, so his visits were filled with curiosity, but he was concerned and interested in all of our preparations. We knew that if ever we needed help with anything, Paul would be there. He was so much like a brother to me. Of course, Aunt Florence always felt that he was part of the family and he had much fondness for her. I know the concerns he felt for her also.

Oregon in fall is a beautiful place to be, with its crisp, cool, mornings and evenings, with the afternoons often too warm for a sweater. We were grateful for this perfect fall day for traveling to St. Helen's Hall, which was located in Portland's Southwest Heights. This was a gorgeous section of Portland at that time. I was wishing, though, that I felt as pretty and comfortable inside as the day was outside. Instead, I was feeling sorry about leaving Sugarpie, even though she loved Aunt Florence. I kept wondering about the kids in Garibaldi, and missing them. I was of course doing nothing more than feeling apprehensive and creating all kinds of fears about this and that. In spite of my feelings, we arrived safe and sound. Uncle Chet had forgotten to be annoyed with all of our luggage. The sisters were so kind and happy to show us to our quarters off the dormitory. The rooms were in a cubicle and we were assigned to a section according to our age group, two girls to a cubicle. Sylvia was in a section for grade school students, so we were separated for the first time. I was completely surprised and astounded. My first thought was, *What will she do at bedtime?* My roommate-to-be was quite a nice girl from eastern Oregon. However, she seemed different, probably because she had attended high school here from the beginning and her mother was an alumni of the Hall. This made me feel more of an outsider than ever. Of course, our bedroom window had bars on it, just exactly as Aunt Ora said it would have. As I glanced from the barred window, I became suddenly curious and interested. There was an open air gymnasium and a handsome tennis court down the one side of the immaculate green grounds. The junior college building went around the property. It reminded me of a picture frame around this attractive courtyard.

Dinnertime was different from home. Instead of a loving voice calling, "Dinner is ready," now there was a dinner bell. In fact, it seemed to me that every move we made was done by a bell. Sister Superior always sat at the head of the table. She couldn't have been more than four-feet-two. She was so tiny, but I learned she was very firm and wise. No one could outdo her at anything. I soon loved her for it! We all held great respect for this little lady. Our dinner table was always covered with white linens, but we had our own linen napkin and napkin ring. For a second I felt close to home as I touched Aunt Florence's name tag on my napkin. When dessert was finished, Sister Superior requested in a cheerful tone that she would enjoy hearing about some of our summer experiences. I wanted so much to tell about our wonderful Alaskan vacation, but I was too shy. Instead, I sat quietly listening to the other girls.

After dinner the girls and one sister left the main brick building for a fun time to be spent across the front lawn in the auditorium. It was a light, friendly building. Immediately, popular dance records were put to use. I was amazed and excited to see how well most of the girls could dance, even though I felt like a klutz, not knowing my left foot from my right. My roommate came to my rescue and began showing me basic dance steps. I was elated! This was wonderful programming by the sisters. It was truly significant because instantly friendship was brought about. There was a feeling of special closeness between the boarders. Many of the girls were from as far away as New York, even China, so the sisters were quite familiar with homesickness. I was fortunate to have Pat Tracy from Dallas attending the Hall, but of course the Sisters made sure we were not living in the same quarters. This was understandable.

Now, we were back in our rooms and I found myself doing as my roommate. She was preparing for bed, so I did the same, being afraid of making a mistake. As I was doing so, Sylvia and a friend ran past our room with Sister Margaret Helena close behind, angrily scolding the two. This upset me. How dare she speak to Sylvia like that! I let her know just exactly how I felt. I learned real quick! You never crossed any of the sisters.

Bedtime came with the sound of a very annoying, irksome bell. It rang through the dorm to encourage the girls to quiet down and prepare for sleep. I had been dreading this point of time from the beginning. What would it be like in this place when it was dark? No Sugarpie to cuddle, no little sister to visit with or tell stories to. Those familiar muffled, lulling sounds the ocean made I was certain to miss more than ever. In spite of my dread and the trepidation, the darkness came and with it came a heavy, deep silence all through the dorm. Through the pale, blue shadows I could see Billy (my roommate) praying on her knees and then crossing herself before crawling into bed. *So strange,* I thought. I wondered if all Episcopalians prayed on their knees. Then my thoughts were interrupted by soft crying and sniffling sounds, so I became aware of homesick girls longing for their families. I cried, not knowing who I was crying for—them or me. Regardless of the tears, I became disgusted with myself! Now Aunt Florence's pillow slip was wet. *Darn me,* I thought to myself.

I was nearing sleep when I suddenly realized the black form of Sister Margaret Helena had appeared. She was checking out and lowering our window and fussed with our blowing, delicate curtain. This surprise visit had startled and struck me as being spooky, but as she was leaving our room, I felt a compassionate, loving touch on my shoulder. I could feel her goodness and, yes, her concerns. For the first time during this long stressful day, I began to feel the pressure of tension leaving. I was so aware of my new nighttime sounds. Instead of the tranquil rhythm

89

of the surf, my new nighttime lullaby became one of an assortment of city tones—the click-clacking of streetcars on their steel tracks and the merry, twinkling jingles they made and the far away deep, throaty whistle of the trains. The swishing of automobiles reminded me of a strong breeze rushing through a tree. All of it together was a lovely nighttime symphony. I thank you, God.

Billy Wade had no idea that she would have a shadow this first day of school. Her name was Nadine Thomas. Yes, I followed her around like a puppy dog. I did everything she did by the bell. We dressed perfectly in our uniforms and our rooms were left in top-notch condition before going to the dining room. Billy warned me, "Be careful about tidiness. You don't want to get orderly marks!" No, I sure didn't want a bad mark. Such a thing sounded gruesome.

Now came the awakening or, you might say, the big blow! It was chapel time, which always came before the beginning of school classes. We were rushed up to the outside of the chapel doors. The girls were all giggly with unbelievable energy and enthusiasm. I felt as though I was in a room full of bees being tossed and pushed from wall to wall. My self-confidence was being shattered and my body became stiff with uneasiness. The unknown was overwhelming. I felt as though I couldn't breathe. Finally, Billy grabbed my arm and pulled me into line. "Here!" she said as she handed me a blue veil for my head. "Tie it on," she ordered. However, she ended up by doing it herself. "Now, I am your partner. We march together in line into the chapel. You must follow the girl in front of you, and do keep your eye on the cross." Billy was firm with her information. Then the chapel doors opened and the organ music poured out, wrapping me with mysterious wonderment. What had happened to my sweet Jesus melodies? But then it was as though I heard my Uncle Chet saying to me, "Step along now." So this I did, as I followed the girl in front of me into the beautiful Episcopalian chapel. I had my first experience of kneeling, standing, sitting, and singing not just hymns but psalms, prayers, and the Apostles' Creed. Everything was sung, even the amens. I then wondered if maybe they couldn't make their minds up because we would no sooner become comfortable sitting when up we would go or down on our knees we went. *Oh well, I have much to learn about all of this,* I was thinking.

The day students filled the chapel's seating area before the service began, so the morning worship commenced with the entry of the boarders. We were the choir, so naturally I perked up with delight over this new awareness. I had never before been in a choir. Another surprise! And a good one for me.

Father Ayers, a large rugged man with a big booming voice to match, was our chaplain. We could not ignore him if we tried. Believe me, he did have our full attention! I was fascinated and intrigued with his heavy, ornate robes. I thought to myself that it was fortunate that he was a large man because the weight of these robes would be difficult for a small man to wear. Our minister at home was lucky. All he had to worry about was his one and only blue serge suit. For some strange reason, I couldn't picture him in this elegant attire. *And wouldn't the folks of Dallas go completely bonkers if he had?* I giggled to myself.

I noticed Sylvia during the service. She was adjusting well, I thought. She and her new friends were getting along as though they had been pals forever. *This is so great,* I thought, *just as long as they can stay out of trouble.* Sylvia and rules never quite jibed. I often thought that Sylvia figured rules were only made to break. Her new friends were all new students, so there was quite an adventure laying ahead. I shuddered thinking about it.

Adjusting to this new way of life was quite arduous for me because of Aunt Ora and her superb method of brainwashing me against this school, probably because I was the oldest. It was all to gain my influence regarding the Tillamook trial. But in spite of all of my negatives and my shyness, I slowly made friends. It all began to happen on the basketball court. My unrestrained enthusiasm for the game soon took over and I became engulfed with zestful friskiness. The older, vigorous and aggressive girls accepted my ability and performance in the game. Ruth from Alaska was one of these students. We became lifelong friends.

I enjoyed chapel every morning. I thought it was a beautiful way to start the day with prayers and music. Father Ayers always had an inspiring lesson for us. How could anyone ever be so smart and wise? I would think. I enjoyed most of my classes but, being a typical teen, I found more pleasure after school hours playing in the gym and learning the game of tennis. I soon learned that the only way a girl was allowed to go outside of the fence was to rescue her tennis ball. One day my ball accidentally hit a spot on the back wall of the gym and out into the street it went. I couldn't believe it at first, but when reality hit me, I was thrilled beyond belief. Out I went! I spotted the ball almost immediately. However, I went through a great deal of dilly-dallying and disguised intentions just to gain a tiny whiff of that sweet free air. I found myself repeating this procedure over and over again. I was outside the court more than once, while the other girls were attempting to mimic my over-the-fence stroke. In the meantime I had become so saturated with weariness and boredom but I decided the game of tennis wasn't that dull after all. In fact, I found myself excited and challenged instead. I was becoming more than just seriously busy with this new game of tennis. I was loving it, as well. I suddenly discovered that I was in a new wonderful world of friends, knowledge, and fun. I realized that all I had to do was to become a part of it. I guess you might say that I was beginning to adjust.

Ah yes, there was discipline and with it, consequences to bear. It was dinner time and with it came lively conversations and soft laughter. It was a happy time. We were all together, resembling a big family, that is, if we didn't get out of line and forget our manners. This evening Sister Superior tapped her water glass with her spoon and with a twinkle in her eye she made it quite clear that she had an announcement to make. The hum of chattering ceased. The dining room became a room of pure silence, not of fear but of respect. Even the maid came to a standstill as Sister was about to speak. "Girls, since we are having such beautiful weather, we have decided to go out to the lake for the weekend. Those of you who would like to go, just sign this paper." I could hardly wait! The mere notion of going to the lake for a whole weekend delighted me beyond words. I was more than just a little elated. I was packed and ready to go hours before our bus was to leave that Friday afternoon. St. Helen's Hall owned a gorgeous lodge out on Lake Oswego. It was only a few miles from Portland. All of the homes surrounding the lake were quite elegant. Some reminded me of mansions and had their own luxurious boats. It was and still is an exclusive area. The clear, cool water was all that I could see and it was so inviting and enticing I was entirely too anxious and bursting with impatience. I had my suit on and I was in the water before anyone could say "Do" or "Don't."

I noticed a rope across a section of the lake. I thought absolutely nothing of it. As I came up, I called to the girls, "Come on in! The water is great." Sister Superior was standing at the edge of the lake. She called to me, "Young lady! You get out and get dressed immediately."

"Sister, what is wrong?" I was completely confused.

"You come here, and I will tell you what is wrong!" she said sharply.

I stood in front of her, wet and shivering. Not from cold but with fright. "What have I done?" I soon found out. I learned very quickly. No one went into the lake without proper supervision, and no one swam past the rope! As I stood there, I felt my frame shrink of discomposure and embarrassment by the minute! "I am sorry, Sister. I didn't know."

"You know now. And just so you don't forget, I am giving you an orderly mark," she said emphatically.

Several of the girls followed me back to the lodge. They were a comfort for both my mental and emotional hurt. I was grateful for their concerns and for helping me gain back a portion of my ego. I spent most of the remaining weekend inside the lodge reading, writing letters, and learning to play Ping-Pong. Swimming inside of the rope was more like playing in a wading pool. It was nothing more than a downer for me. Sister invited several of us to ride in her boat, which was powered by an outboard motor. It was fun, and I felt good inside that she invited me to join in for the ride. I was surprised as to how this tiny sister could manipulate such a large motor with her sleeves rolled up to her elbows and her black habit flying in the wind. As we flew past the elegant home of the Janitzens, the Jantzen boys came out in their speedboat, making waves so that our boat would rock and roll. Sister was somewhat ruffled as some of the girls squealed and screamed, but wrong as it was, I couldn't help but think how funny it would have been if all of us were dumped into the lake beyond that discriminating rope. Of course, it didn't happen and we returned to the lodge as dry as when we had left.

As I jumped from the boat, Sister gave my backside a weak swat, but with a smile, probably because I didn't squeal. *Or did she read my mind?* I wondered. It was a love swat, that was for sure, because from that day forward we were the best of friends. However, my orderly mark was still on the agenda so I spent the next Saturday in the study hall instead of going out to lunch and to the movies with the other chaperoned girls.

Going out to lunch and to the movies was the treat for the week, even if it had to be with a chaperone. Upperclassmates were allowed to leave the campus on their own and they could go most anytime they wished. *Wonderful to be sixteen,* I thought. Saturday movies and lunch spent in downtown Portland was thought about and planned for all during the week by the girls. Sundays were different. They could be a lonely, forlorn day and so long and drawn out if we didn't find something interesting to do. Of course, Sunday morning always began by marching to church. I use the word "march" because after we passed Sister's inspection, which was to be dressed properly with hats and gloves and with little or no make-up, we would line up in pairs. Yes indeed, we would march to church with two sisters behind all of the assembled girls as if they were herding us as good shepherds. So we "marched" to church. Under my breath I would automatically hum *Glory, Glory, Hallelujah!* until our jazzy steps arrived to the majestic, St. Stephen's Episcopal Church. The service was a tremendous bore except for the music, and not all of that was pleasing for me. The minister didn't hold a candle to Father Ayers, I thought, so I squirmed. What a blessing for me that there was kneeling and standing. I enjoyed watching the alter boys, which helped break the monotony. I was intrigued watching senior girls delightfully flirt with handsome young men in the congregation. I always wondered if maybe they might meet someday.

Sunday afternoon blues, in time, were overcome with tennis, books, and writing letters. I found a great deal of amusement in making up and writing stories. I had a fun time, too, creating a series. The girls were entertained also. They would wait with curiosity and enthusiasm for my finale. My stories almost always were love stories. We younger girls had another mischievous pastime: we loved to spy on the older girls and their visiting boyfriends. "You kids just wait! You will have your turn!" they'd say.

"No way will I ever have a boyfriend. It's silly and yucky," I would say. Little did I know.

Sunday evening Father Ayers held a small service in our chapel called "Eve'n Song." It was gratifying and a very pretty Sunday evening event, especially given for the boarders. Father Ayers always had a wholesome message for us. How I loved the music and sharing with my own voice. The flickering and glowing candlelight intensified the spiritual beauty of the chapel.

Sylvia seemingly was enjoying the Hall and her new friends. Every time we would see one another she appeared to be busy and happy about everything. This alone was a relief and pleasing for me, and, too, I had not heard of any mischief. "Thank you, Father, for keeping Sylvia away from trouble." I no sooner had given my thanks when, lo and behold, I had a visit from Sister Margaret Helena.

"Tell me, Nadine, has Sylvia ever walked in her sleep?" she asked me.

I was dumbfounded and I wondered what on earth was going on. I didn't know if I should fib, keeping her out of trouble, or be honest and say what I finally did. "No, Sister, she has never been a sleepwalker, not to my knowledge." I said, while still wondering what on Earth was going on.

"Well, she walked into my room after lights were out last night and I had to walk her back to her room," Sister informed me.

I could tell that she was concerned and disturbed. I was flabbergasted! What on Earth was Sylvia thinking about? I was absolutely furious with her. What a dumb stunt, and I knew it was a stunt. That afternoon I got hold of her. "Sylvia, what on Earth were you doing in Sister Margaret's room?"

"Oh, I just wanted to see what the sisters wore at night," she said to me in a very unconcerned tone.

"Well, it is none of your business!" I said with so much anger. "You should be punished plenty." I don't believe that she was ever punished. The sisters knew I would have a heated discussion with her and heated it was! I am certain that if she had been a sleepwalker she would have been sent home. Thank goodness I told the truth.

It was Halloween season and with it came an invitation to Hill Military Academy's Halloween party and dance. The girls were all in a twitter, really fired up, you might say, as to what dress to wear or "Should I change my hairstyle?" On and on! Our dorm was sounding much like a beehive! There was much excitement. Me? Well, I could not imagine dancing with a boy, let alone a strange one. It didn't help, either, to be lacking in self-confidence regarding my dancing ability. The older girls gave me a boost regarding my self-assurance. During our after dinner dancing they came forth with needed praise. "You'll do just fine. Just relax and be yourself." My heart was in my throat just the same the night of my first dance. Before we were to leave for the Academy, we all were to gather in the main entrance with Sister Superior. She was more than fussy about how we should be dressed. She must approve of each one of us. Heaven forbid if light should shine through our skirts, so each one of us had to walk in front of her blazing spotlight. I was thankful indeed that she couldn't see through my taffeta skirt. Too bad for us if she could see down the front of our neckline. I wondered what was next, but that was it. We were merrily on our way!

Before I knew it, we had arrived at the dance hall and lined up like debutantes waiting to be escorted by a military uniformed partner. I felt so elegant with my arm folded into my escort's arm as we walked to the dance floor. We both were consoled when the band played a soft, slow waltz. I knew how he felt when he said, "Oh, I do know how to waltz." I couldn't have asked for a better beginning. My partner was nice-looking and taller than me. He enjoyed talking about his folks and their eastern Oregon ranch. I could tell that he loved and missed his home, so I became a good listener, as the older girls instructed, but I had to tell him about my clam-digging and other coastal experiences. With my eyes sparkling. I described my beautiful lake.

Since this was a Halloween party, we were delighted to have a Gypsy fortuneteller included. I was excited about that and was even more thrilled to receive a good fortune. The dance hall was decorated with bright orange and black crepe paper streamers and balloons. We had ice cream with orange cookies. This was my first real honest-to-goodness Halloween party with not only a wonderful beginning, but a wonderful ending as well.

It was difficult to simmer down Monday morning for chapel as there was still an air of exuberance among all the girls. It was difficult to calm and compose our thoughts toward the old routine. Still, there was talk and more talk about the Saturday night party. We sounded more like a flock of jay-birds in spite of the school bell! As we were all waiting outside of the chapel doors, I could see this service was to be different. The boarders were not going to sing in the choir; instead, we were to sit with the day students. I noticed the cross was draped with a black chiffon cloth. *This is so strange. And why?* I wondered. "What is going on?" I whispered to one of the girls.

"This is just All Souls Day." She was quite nonchalant about the entire occurrence so I guessed it wasn't too big of a deal! I would do as I had done before: I just would do as they did. I had a very strange sensation go through me as I walked into the chapel behind the black covered cross. The organ was playing such heavy, dark tones, sounds of an unwholesome feeling. I wanted to cover my ears from this sullen, melancholic music, but of course, I didn't. Instead, I kneeled and prayed with the other girls. As I glanced up at the altar, I could see it, too, was draped in black. I was surprised to see Father Ayers clad in black robes as well. In a hushed tone I said to the girl next to me, "What are we doing?"

"We are blessing the dead," she whispered softly. I became extremely uncomfortable. It became so cold in there and I was shaking. My throat was in pain from pressing back sobs of grief. I was crying inside for my mother and dad. How I wished I could be like the other girls. My heart was breaking all over again. *How many times can my heart break?* I wondered. I held on to myself until the lady soloist sang. It was so beautiful but so very sad and heavyhearted I went to pieces, sobbing violently.

Sister Margaret Helena grabbed me and literally dragged me from the chapel. She shook me with such force, I thought my neck would break. She said over and over again, "You straighten up right now or you can start packing your things. I will be glad to call your uncle to come get you." She took me back to my room. "You think about what I said. And I mean it. You straighten up, or go home. Now stay in your room until you have made up your mind. One way or the other." I stayed in my room, sitting in my chair, stunned and staring out of the window. I knew that I couldn't leave Sylvia. What would Aunt Florence and Uncle Chet do with me? I knew I was stuck. *How dare Sister treat me like this,* I thought. *I hate this school! I don't ever want to go back into that awful chapel!* I wanted to throw things, but I didn't. I walked the floor instead, thinking *What am I going to do? I know what you are going to do. You are going to wash your face, pick up your books, and go to class. You know well that you don't hate anyone or anything about this school and you are not a quitter. So straighten up.* That little inner voice had spoken. I rinsed my face in cold water and went on to my morning classes with my head held high! I didn't stay long, did I, whale?

There was nothing I enjoyed more than that hour of choir practice. However, I tried not to display my enthusiasm too much because most of the girls disliked giving up their free time to something as dull as choir practice. Heaven forbid I should be thought of as a weirdo, but I couldn't help feeling so tingly and happy inside to just open my mouth and make such gorgeous sounds! However, the Episcopalian music was a flawless mystery for me. I wished so much that practice would last a few minutes longer. Maybe then, I would comprehend more about this exotic, alluring music. There were times I felt as though I was in a fog. Would I ever get it? I was so discouraged. Then there was a miracle! It was as through a lightbulb had just lit! I had it! What a delight, and how great it was! I sang those phrases as though I was bursting inside. What an exciting triumph! Sister Agatha Louise was our choir director who also, in fact, managed and controlled the school's entire music department. She was such a pretty, feminine lady who had a swing to her walk. I thought many times that her spirit surely was one of music. I said to her one day, "Sister, do you know you dance instead of walk?"

She just laughed and said, "I guess I got caught. I didn't think that anyone noticed." And oh! Her eyes! Whenever someone mentions blue eyes, even today, I immediately think of Sister Agatha Louise. She had without a doubt the most beautiful blue eyes ever. She was my favorite sister, and I am sure it was because of her love and knowledge of music, beautiful music. She could make you sad or make you laugh with her music. I adored just being where she was. When she called to me this special day, I thought, *Oh good, Sister wants to speak with me.*

When she began saying, "Nadine, I have been wondering. Have you ever thought about taking private voice lessons?" I was a little shocked by her question.

"Well, I guess maybe I have because I do want to be a good singer. My mother wanted this for me."

"Well, I'll tell you what I am going to do. I will write to your uncle and aunt and suggest that you have private voice lessons. Mrs. Hilderbrant is a marvelous professional voice instructor. We think one of the best. In the meantime you have our permission to use the music room any time you want to use it." Sister Agatha Louise left me speechless. I was numb with excitement as my secret thoughts were unfolding.

Chapter Fourteen

My new world in boarding school was becoming one big adventure. I enjoyed almost everything it had to offer. I must have unknowingly accepted the bars on the windows and never having permission to venture outside of the fence without a chaperone. The once irritating sound of those demanding bells didn't faze me in the least. I didn't have time to become resentful. There were so many new challenging activities along with the old to become fascinated with. It all was very wonderful. All of the girls were my friends. There was not one girl that I disliked. You might say we stuck together, but there was plenty of mischief along with concerns and the capacity for sharing in the interests of one another, compassion, and empathy.

Pat, my Dallas friend, could not eat her tomato aspic salad, "It will gag me," she kept telling Sister Superior, which didn't make any difference. Pat must eat her salad, and that was that! She was not allowed to leave the dining room until she had finished the salad. Poor Pat was left completely alone in that large silent room. One by one the girls would sneak down to the dining room and give encouragement and rally her on to victory. There were tears and gagging, but finally she made it. Yes, we were all close to one another but it is quite natural to have one favorite friend. My closest friend was dear Ruth from Fairbanks, Alaska. Our friendship began with our love of basketball. She was a tall, athletic girl and also quite a brilliant student. She was in her junior year so she had special privileges, which irritated me a little. She was the badminton champion for Alaska. Try and try again, my efforts were thwarted, but she never beat me at tennis! We were quite a pair! We both made the basketball team. I didn't dream that I would make it, as I was the youngest, and only five feet, five inches.

The day finally arrived when Sister Agatha Louise came bursting forth with thrilling news. She couldn't wait to tell me as she called out from the end of the long hall, "Your uncle gave his permission for singing lessons!" I was so relieved but must have felt just a little apprehensive. I really would be taking voice lessons. How wonderful, wonderful! I was introduced to Mrs. Hilderbrant the next day and immediately began my lessons. I liked her even though I felt shy and timid. She gave me a song to sing, then said, "My, how come so weak? You must not be the girl I heard during chorus practice with the big voice." I soon learned about vocal exercising, one right after another. And for some crazy reason I thought about Herman. Wouldn't he have had a ball sitting through one of these sessions! I began to feel relaxed and very determined to do well with this talent of mine. I wanted more than anything to have Uncle Chet and Aunt Florence be proud of me. I was pleased to learn that Uncle Chet wanted Sylvia to also have some musical training. She chose piano lessons and did quite well, but whether she enjoyed it or not, I was never quite sure.

Even though we both were happy and in harmony with our new school, we were thrilled to go home for our first holiday, Thanksgiving. We could hardly wait. I almost made myself sick by becoming overly excited. As I look back, I think we must have driven the folks dizzy with our chatter, especially Aunt Florence. *There is no place like home,* I thought. *How glorious and comfy my own bed is going to feel.* It was heavenly to hold Sugarpie. "Aunt Florence, what have you done to her? She is so beautiful," I said.

She just smiled with tongue in cheek. "Well, she has been combed and brushed every day, that's what!"

I managed an embarrassing, "Oh!"

Now, of course air is air; however, while walking up main street this was the sweetest air I had ever smelled. I filled my lungs full of it. I felt like singing, perhaps I did. I felt so carefree and happy-go-lucky. I never thought of freedom as something to hold and to hold on to.

Thanksgiving morning was brimming and overflowing with the exciting expectancy of seeing relatives. The delicious aroma escaping from Aunt Florence's kitchen was driving us all wild and creating negative impatience. "Will the turkey be done on time?"

"Oh, I pray that it will," Aunt Florence said, reassuring herself. Of course it was roasted perfect, and on time. Everything about her Thanksgiving table was eloquent and with all of the brilliance and warmth of Thanksgiving. The Tillamook folks all came, as well as Ivy with her man friend, so there was plenty of laughter and pleasant conversation. How important I felt when Aunt Florence would ask me to help refill our crystal water goblets or add more to this or that. It was her saying "Our goblets" that reminded me that this was our home and our Thanksgiving table! I was embraced with thankfulness. Ah yes, I was puffed up with self-esteem. Sylvia and I had a place to belong to, a home like other kids had.

I believed that this was the first Thanksgiving dinner where there hadn't been a political discussion. I no sooner thought it when an argument flared. *Oh boy! Here we go!* I thought. I could tell that Uncle Chet was getting angry and Aunt Ada's face was getting red. *There is going to be an awful argument,* I was thinking, *and Uncle Chet needs help. Everyone is against him except Uncle Roy, and he won't say anything.* So I said, "You know that in six months Uncle Chet will prove he is right." Uncle Roy choked on his pumpkin pie while Aunt Jessie gave me a quick glare of disapproval, but Uncle Chet smiled from ear to ear. I said later to Aunt Florence. "It just slipped out, Aunt Florence. I didn't mean to be disrespectful."

"Well, your Uncle Roy was more than a little amused. You know, you really made his day," Aunt Florence said with a chuckle. "You know, don't you, that you did end an argument. By the way, Nadine, thank you for filling your Uncle Frank's water glass. I hope you realize that you have taken a big step."

The long weekend at home was as perfect as they come, as was the celebrated Thanksgiving. Just to be home was an indescribable treat! Before leaving for school, the folks read a letter to us from the school saying that at the beginning of the year lessons were being offered at Timberline for skiing and also that the Highland riding academy would be giving lessons for horseback riding. Uncle Chet said that we could take just one, we couldn't have both. Sylvia knew immediately that it was skiing she wanted. Now, I had one awful time trying to make up my mind. I wanted both. One day it would be skiing, the next day it would be the horses. I finally decided on the horses, so another adventure would soon begin with a new year.

St. Helen's Hall was one of wonderment for me all through the month of December. The love of Christmas was moving our minds and lifting our spirits. Happiness was everywhere. It was also the busiest time of the year, especially for Sister Agatha Louise. Since music was her specialty, she could more than do her marvelous giving of it during the Christmas season. A beautiful Christmas cantata was her gift, to be presented the night before our Christmas vacation. The boarders were the ones who sang and acted the cantata for her. The new girls were always the angels (the chorus), so the leading roles were assigned to the upper grades. The angel Gabriel was the leading role. We practiced hard and long, and over and over again. Sister Agatha Louise was a perfectionist without a doubt. It wasn't until the night of our dress rehearsal that I realized how gorgeous and magnificent this musical was. Our stage became a holiday inspiration for all to see—the beautiful white angels with glittering silver halos and wings, Mary in her blue with Joseph by her side.

In the center, and above all of the others, was the majestic angel Gabriel, adorned in a scarlet robe. "Her" halo and wings were lustrous, glowing gold. (In a girls' school, Gabriel had to be a girl.) I was spellbound among all of this Christmas beauty. I now understood Sister Agatha Louise! This music must be sung with only eloquence and beauty, and most important of all, with feeling. It must be as perfect as we could make it. The night of the cantata we became a group of serious, big-eyed, quiet girls, not saying a word, except a scant whisper now and then. So much anticipation, the air was full of it!

"Now, girls, it is time to give our Christmas gift of music," Sister Agatha Louise said as the stage curtain parted. We were beautiful creating a breathtaking scene more spectacular than any Christmas card could ever express. When the music began, our anticipation lessened into a full expression of the Christmas spirit. I sang with the angels while pretending that I was one. As I glanced down into the audience, I could see Uncle Chet clearly. He was sitting proudly in the front row. How I wanted to wave, hoping he could see me. I intentionally did a squirming act instead. When the angel Gabriel sang her obbligato to the *Cantique de-Noel,* and the angels sang in the background, everyone in the auditorium was completely enchanted. Oh, how thrilled I was with this piece of music. I wished and dreamed to sing her part more than anything else in the whole world. It was as though my mother was saying, "You can do it." I told myself that night, *I am going to be her in my senior year.* I became excited with my new expectation. Only God knows my secret!

Sylvia and I were packed and more than ready for home since we were to leave as soon as the program came to an end. "Uncle Chet, did you see us on the stage tonight?" I anxiously inquired.

"I saw an angle that had a crooked halo. Was that one you?" He hurt my feelings, but my feelings recovered because of so much Christmas excitement bouncing around inside of me. I wondered if Aunt Florence would have a Christmas tree in the house. She never liked the mess they made. Maybe it would be different this year, and it was!

Christmas, Christmas! I had never experienced one before or since to equal it! There was a beautiful gorgeous tree with twinkling, perfectly placed tree lights with gifts heaped high under it. "Merry Christmas, girls!" Aunt Florence cheerfully called out to us as we bounced into the house with Uncle Chet close behind. I was flabbergasted with wondrous surprise. This festive greeting, I believe, we all dream about. We both were mesmerized and neither one of us could speak. Aunt Florence said later, "Your eyes did the talking for you!"

I thought it was a little strange that our unique tree only had lights on it without any other ornaments until Uncle Chet said, "Now, when I was a kid we strung popcorn and cranberries for our tree." So the next evening we three sat in front of our living room fireplace with a box of cranberries and an equal amount of popcorn. And, mind you, we were not going anyplace until this project was accomplished. Our high-handed Uncle Chet, Sylvia, and I worked like beavers stabbing our fingers with the needles as well. Paul stopped by out of curiosity, I'm sure. He could see the three of us through the big living room window. He had to see for himself.

"Well, stringing popcorn...huh. Haven't seen that done for years," Paul said.

"Well, now you have. Pull up a chair and join us," Uncle Chet said.

Paul left with a twinkle in his eye and Aunt Florence finally came to our rescue. "I really think this will be enough. There are other ornaments to go on the tree also." I am sure she saved his evening as well as ours but now, when I look back at this night, it had to be a joyous time for all four of us. These two people were making our first Christmas together as perfect as possible for us. How wonderful it was for them also. This was their first Christmas tree to be enjoyed by not only us, but by them as well. No wonder our dear friend Paul just had to drop by. He had to see for himself our very distinguished Uncle Chet stringing cranberries and popcorn.

The next day we carefully placed each ornament in a perfect showy position and gracefully arranged the valuable strings of popcorn and cranberries as though they were precious rubies and diamonds. Our tree was one of exceptional beauty, Sylvia and I both agreed as we stood back and admired our work of art. Uncle Chet was feeling quite kittenish this evening and decided that there was nothing like a little nip from the bourbon bottle to bring about even more cheer. "Okay," we all agreed. "Now is the time to turn on the tree's lights!" We had waited long enough, so the four of us, full of anticipation, went into the sunroom where our tree was waiting to reveal her beauty. We were more than ready to turn on the tree lights when Uncle Chet decided to do a little jig. Then suddenly his feet went out from under him! Our gorgeous tree went bonkers with him. "Our tree, our tree!" Sylvia and I were horrified as Uncle Chet and the tree twirled and swirled together! Finally he made a spectacular landing in the middle of the room with the finely decorated tree successfully sprawled on top. Sylvia and I could think of nothing except our concerns for the tree. Aunt Florence, well, she was in a state of uncontrollable laughter. For days, just the mention of Chet and the tree would set her off! Uncle Chet was not hurt—only his pride, and that was bad enough! Sugarpie left for safer ground.

Our Christmas was beautiful in every way with friends and relatives sharing our joys and love for Christmas. It was amazing to me the abundance of friends Aunt Florence had attracted to her. It reminded me of moths to a flame. "Oh my goodness, here comes the town's gossip. She just wants to see for herself that the Henkles have a Christmas tree," Aunt Florence said with disgust. She was right, as Mrs. Henery instantly walked straight to the sunroom.

"Well, I heard right. Mr. Henkle does have a tree this year. It's hard to believe," she said.

There is nothing as remarkable as words from the mouths of babes. With folded arms and a determined tone, Sylvia said, "That is right. Uncle Chet has waited for years for just the perfect tree. And this was the year that he found one."

"That is right, Mrs. Henery," Aunt Florence said.

Christmas Eve was our gift-giving night, shared with Ivy and her soon-to-be husband. Sylvia and I were showered with presents, so it was natural to be overwhelmed. I remember asking Aunt Florence if I could please sit in Grandma's chair for just a minute or so? I was paralyzed with the abundance of gift-giving, so out of the way I sat in the tiny chair before opening another present. Now, I could breath. Strange as it seems, the tiny chair was almost like magic! (Which was a blessing because my next gift was a eye-popping experience.) Inside of this gorgeous box was a pair of shiny, elegant, black riding boots. I became numb by this marvelous unexpectedness. "You are ready now for Black Beauty," Aunt Florence said. I was glad that she could say something, because I was speechless!

After Christmas came to an end, Uncle Chet took his family to California. What a thrill to see my first palm tree and the orange and olive orchards. We were all eyes during these next few days. San Francisco, I do believe was my favorite part of the trip. In those days there were beautiful, fragrant flower carts seemingly on every corner. The excitement and the fun fisherman's wharf, clearly conveyed, brought so much enjoyment. I disliked leaving San Francisco to go on down south. However, it did become another great experience. Horse racing at Santa Anita, dinner at The Brown Derby, and of course the famous Tournament of Roses parade was indeed a thrill to see. Aunt Florence had relatives living in Beverly Hills, so nothing else would do. We had to have dinner at their home. It was a fabulous home, resembling a Hollywood mansion. I am sure Aunt Florence was somewhat uncomfortable because she was not sure about our manners. As soon as we left she couldn't wait to say, "Girls, your manners were impeccable. I was so tickled you both knew how to use your finger bowl,"

"Oh, Aunt Florence, we have finger bowls all of the time at school," I said in a very matter-of-fact way. She was spellbound with our lady-like manners. And this made us pleased. We had not bothered to tell her that once a week we were given a class in manners. I laugh now, as she must have thought we just might drink from the finger bowl!

We no sooner arrived back home from California when it was time to pack up again and leave for school. This time, leaving was with happy, anxious feelings. I was eager to see the girls, especially Ruth, and to get back into the swing of things, most importantly, my voice lessons.

When I think back today, I realize the ultimate exposure we were given to see and hear the greatest of the famous and most celebrated musicians of the world. When the sisters mentioned season tickets to Uncle Chet, he didn't bat an eye. We were to have tickets for all of the concerts. There are not enough words to express how very fortunate we were to see and hear these fantastic artists. So many of them are gone today, such as Nelson Eddy, Lawrence Tibbits, Grace Moore, Marion Anderson, and John Charles Thomas. There were scores of others, so this was another happy reason for returning to school—the concerts. There was always a brilliant artist to look forward to and enjoy.

Music? There wasn't enough of it! I was in another world with every one of the concerts. When the lights dimmed, the curtain raised, and the music commenced, I was thankful that I was the only one who could hear and feel my heart pound or feel the bumps on my skin. Thank goodness no one could see my tears the night I heard Marion Anderson sing *Ave Maria*. It was as though she left forever lasting fingerprints on my heart.

Again, we walked in pairs, followed usually by two chaperones, to the civic auditorium (uptown Portland) for the given concert. Returning was cheerful, with lively steps. It was such fun to sing and hum songs from the concert and then step in time with our music. Those poor chaperones did have a time. They gained a workout, that's for sure. The Bush Drugstore was a "must stop" before returning back to school. There never has been another soda fountain that could make a more perfect hot fudge sundae. Not to my knowledge! I'll bet the Bushes would make the same comment about the girls from St. Helen's Hall. "What energy! What overflowing enthusiasm. No one could outdo them." They must have given thanks when we all left!

My voice lessons began with more zest and stronger drive from Mrs. Hilderbrant after returning from Christmas vacation. I was delighted with new songs to learn and not just vocalize. I was surprised Sister Agatha Louise wanted me to become familiar with new hymns for the choir. Mrs. Hilderbrant informed me that because my voice was strong, the other girls were inclined to follow me. I was enjoying my singing lessons, though at times I was just a little leery of her. I knew that she had a temper. I saw her dark eyes flash more than once. The day she slammed the piano keyboard cover down with a bang, she scared me stiff. With tears, I was ready to quit right there and then. I didn't even wait to gather up my music. I only had one thought and that was to leave. She called to me, shamefaced. "Nadine, I am sorry. You must understand, sometimes you just infuriate me because you do exactly what I tell you to do, and I can't begin to do what I am teaching you," she said, as she began to cry. I did not understand what she was trying to explain to me. I only felt confused and sorry for her. Maybe she was only having a rotten day, so I gathered up my composure and as she calmed down we carried on with my lesson. From then on we had a special kinship.

The days almost were not long enough with my studies, choir practice, basketball, voice lessons, and now once a week there were horseback riding lessons. These lessons were more difficult than I had ever dreamed. Just getting on and off was more of an arduous manipulation than I had ever imagined. As a matter of fact, I never once gave it a thought. I almost wished I had decided upon skiing lessons rather than going for the horses, especially when I first stood beside the horse I was soon to mount. He appeared enormous. *He must be oversized,* I was thinking. I looked over at Pat and wondered if I looked as pale as she surely did. One thing about it, we both were in the same boat—scared to death. But it was amazing that in a few weeks we both were truly riding and the fear was slowly but surely becoming one of pleasure in spite of our rear ends. I suffered with deep blisters and flesh wounds in and about the inner part of my knees. Learning to ride an English saddle takes a great deal of endurance. Believe me, it was no picnic! But how grateful and thankful I have been through the years to know and appreciate the art of horseback riding. My friend Pat and I spent many joyful hours riding around the captivating wooded areas and hills of Dallas. What a glorious time we had. It was this enchanting pleasure we shared that became a treasure of mine.

It was nearing spring and with spring would come a visit from Mother Superior. So much chatter about this and that and the other thing, everything must be perfect, and shined to the hilt! I was curious about her, but that was about the extent of it for me. Sister Margaret Helena approached me and asked if I would consider singing a solo in a program that they had planned for Mother Superior. I was dumbfounded and a little horrified. "Why me, Sister? Surely someone else would be a better choice," was my answer.

"Well, you think about it," she said. After listening to another pupil who has been studying much longer than I had with Mrs. Hilderbrant, I was deeply concerned. *If I sound as bad as she does. I will never sing in public again. So the sisters better get someone else,* I thought. I decided, no way!

The girls, especially Ruth started in on me. "You must sing. The sisters are really counting on you." The girls began to shame me.

"You don't understand," I said. "Look at Marie. She has been studying for years. And look at her. She sounds awful. So, if anything, I must sound even worse. I'm not going to get up there and make a fool of myself."

It was quite obvious that the girls had told Sister why I was refusing to sing because she came back to me. "Nadine, we understand that you don't want to sing because you don't think you are good enough. Is that right?"

"That is right. Maybe in another year, I'll consider singing." Both Mrs. Hilderbrant and Sister wouldn't let me refuse. They won out with their argument. I decided to appease them and sing in the program. I thought it was exciting when they told me that I could sing whatever I wanted to, and that Mrs. Hilderbrant would be happy to help. I was especially fond of *Love Walked Right In. Oh, I would love to sing that song.* The more I thought about it the more thrilled I became. Mrs. Hilderbrant explained to me, "Marie has been learning to sing. Now you can sing, and this is fortunate, but your voice needs a lot of hard work. Believe me, you do have plenty to learn." I felt ashamed of my critical behavior regarding Marie's voice, another good lesson learned to help get along in this old, wise world.

Mrs. Hilderbrant was being gracious and generous with her time coaching me for the program. She laughed and teased me one day when she said, "You could use a little more feeling when you sing this song. I'll tell you what. Just think of your boyfriend while doing this number." She didn't know, but it was as though she had just lit a spark in my heart. Suddenly, I remembered that heart-throbbing sensation I experienced the day I saw Larry, so long ago. The feeling was indescribable, so I sang *Love Walked Right In* and I clearly sent my romantic emotions soaring.

"That's it! You are ready for the program!"

I had such support and encouragement from all of the girls the night of the program. They were all there in the front row, ready to cheer me on. After Mother Superior was introduced, several talks were given by the sisters, telling about Mother Superior. My, I had no idea she was such an important lady from New York and New Jersey. I was getting just a tad bit nervous and wishing this evening was over. The minutes were beginning to seem like hours. The longer I sat, the harder my heart pounded! Finally, Sister Superior introduced me and Mrs. Hilderbrant as she approached the piano. The girls gave me a terrific boost with a rip-roaring applause, but I didn't settle down until I heard the melody of my song. My emotions changed into happy, lighthearted feelings, bringing with them a joyful, sunny song. The audience applauded wildly while I experienced an ecstatic thrill that encompassed my entire body.

We were all enjoying our cookies and punch after the program was over when Sister Margaret Helena tapped me on the shoulder and asked me to come over to the parlor as soon as I finished with my refreshments. I wondered, *What now?* as very seldom were we invited to the parlor, unless we'd done something wrong. Anticipation got the better of me, so I left instantly for the parlor. I was astounded to see Mother Superior sitting alone, waiting for me in this pretentiously decorated room. She directed me to sit beside her in one of the luxurious chairs. There was a very warm, softness about her. *What an elegant lady she is,* I thought. But there was a way about her that made me feel quite comfortable and at ease while close to her. I wasn't at all self-conscious, as I might have been. "I know you must be wondering why I have sent for you. I especially want to thank you for your singing tonight and to tell you how much I enjoyed your stunning, cheerful song. You do have a lovely voice, dear, and I pray that you will take care of it and continue on with your voice lessons. It would be so wonderful if you would go to New York to study your music. I know all of the best schools. If you decided upon a musical career, I want you to know that I would be pleased if you would contact me." I was overwhelmed. I couldn't believe that it was me she was talking to!

Here comes Ash Wednesday! As new girls we heard plenty about the pancakes rolled in ashes. Of course, I didn't believe it, but there is always that little speck of apprehension. Could it be true? One thing about it, if we did have real ashes in our pancakes, we jolly well better eat them or spend the night in the dining room until we did. I was skittish hearing about the Friday night mudpies also. "You'll have to eat them too, Nadine, or get an orderly mark." The mudpies were a delicious surprise. They didn't resemble a pie at all. My first reaction was that they must have changed the menu. They were white cupcakes, not pie. The girls cut a hole in the center of the cake and poured chocolate sauce over the cake. I watched intently, then I copied the maneuver with the greatest of interest. Of course, the chocolate syrup turned the cupcakes into mudpies. Every bite was a marvelous, delicious experience. I thought I was in heaven for sure. So now it was time for the ash-pancakes. I waited with concern and curiosity. The wait was more than worthwhile. The pancakes were warm and had been rolled in powdered sugar! It was indeed a delightful delicacy. It was worth the long curiosity-filled wait. The whale and I had been playing a game with one another all day long.

Chapter Fifteen

My thoughts were miles away as I was sauntering down the hallway when Sister Margaret Helena's arm went around my waist. I was startled at first because I didn't realize she was near. "Nadine, I want to speak to you about Lent. The sisters and I have been talking and we all agree that you shouldn't give up food for Lent. Most of the girls do, you know, but it might be harmful for you. You can fulfill your religious penitence in other ways, dear," she said as my heart sank. I wanted to give up desserts and be like the other girls.

"Sister, I am as healthy as any of the other girls, "I said as she left me standing there alone with a long face.

"We plan on keeping you that way," she called back lauging. *Okay,* I thought. *Well, I can study harder in study hall, instead of wasting time. That is it. That will be my repentance.* At the end of my forty days God rewarded me with better grades...and I was not one pound heavier.

Now came the Easter weekend. I was just sixteen so I was old enough to spend this beautiful religious festival there at school. Sylvia went home for the weekend, which was the first time we had been separated. I felt grown up about it and and yet it was sad for me and brought a tear.

The Easter weekend began the Thursday before Easter. I knew we were to go into silence that very evening but couldn't fathom what it might belike, so I deliberately kept my thoughts clear of it, knowing I might become fearful of the unknown. I was determined to keep mu silence, and receive a pin for doing so. That was that! I had convinced myself.

The bell rang just before dinner and with it our silencce began. The large school building suddenly became heavy with a dead of stillness. Becoming voiceless resembled the silence of a tomb. There was not a sound from a single person. I glanced over at the other girls, and their reactions must have been similar to my amazed feelings. Ruth's eyes were as big as silver dollars. I swear her hair was standing on end. When the dinnerbell rang, I almost jumped out of my skin. Ruth slammed her hand over her mouth because she almost spoke. We huddled close to one another while walking to the dining room. Our footsteps sounding more like a herd of buffalo than steps of teenage girls. I was surprised as we walked passed the hallway clock as to how loud it ticked. Every sound heard was magnified. After the silent blessing was given, I was dumbfounded to hear that awful scraping noise our chairs made as we were preparing to seat ourselves. And the rumbling, dinging, clattering from our silver and china was almost enough to send us into orbit. By this time there wasn't one girl who didn't have an urge to laugh. I was in sheer agony attempting to control my laughter. I couldn't look into the face of one girl. If I had, I'm sure I would have gone into hysterics.

I was delighted to see that we were having roast beef and crispy, browned potatoes served for our dinner. My favorite dinner, I do believe! While I was eagerly attempting to cut my potato into a bite-sized piece, it suddenly developed what seemed like a wing and flew clear across the table. At first we all sat there in perfect amazement, not believing our eyes! But then there wasn't one of us who could keep a straight face, including Sister Superior. Her tiny round face resembled a ripe tomato. Not one of us made a sound.

After dinner we prepared ourselves for an evening walk, first by assembling ourselves in pairs with Sister Elizabeth Marion bringing up the rear. What an odd, strange sensation, walking in silence excpet for the thudding sound of footsteps. Of course, the residents of the neighborhood were fascinated and some were downright curious and questioned this strange procedure, especially when we ignored their polite "Good Evenings" or "Isn't this a beautiful evening for a walk?" I realized several of the girls were amused, but I felt nothing other than embarrassment and uneasiness. I became even more humiliated when at first a small boy appeared on the scene, then there were two. In no time at all we were surrounded by gawking, snoopy children. One boy delighted himself by hiding behind shrubs, then jumping out at us while making ugly faces. Another young man amused himself by sticking out his vulgar tongue, just for our benefit. Poor Sister must have been beside herself with frustration, especially when a small white, barking terrier appeared at her heels. I felt nothing but contempt for this so-called "Good for the soul walk and wished we were back at school. I must not have been alone with these thoughts because our steps were becoming faster and faster. Sister was at least a towering six feet tall, so it took two steps from us to equal her one rapid stride. Thank heavens, we soon were back at school, with Sister Elizabeth Marion waving her arms at Sister Superior, and without humor!

Good Friday began in the chapel, on our knees and without breakfast and, of course, in silence. Two of the girls became sick and when one girl fainted, I had a feeling I would be next because I had a horrible sensation of swimming and my head was hot and then icy cold. The next thing I knew Sister Margaret Helena was escorting me from the chapel. I was grateful to be back in my room, but I would be more than just grateful to have all of this behind me.

The next big affair of the day was a special elaborate luncheon given especially for the bishop, alumni, and other distinguished guests. It was wonderful that we could enjoy this delicious, fancy luncheon, even though we had to wait until last. For the first time we were happy about the silence: Now we couldn't be expected to carry on polite, lighthearted conversations with unknown guests. It was a yummy out-of-this-world treat.

After the luncheon was over, we were on our own to do as we

wished while maintaining our silence. Because I was now sixteen, I could leave the campus without a chaperone, so Ruth and I decided to go to the Bush Pharmacy and have one of their scrumptious hot fudge sundaes. We knew we deserved something special besides the enjoyment of this beautiful, warm spring day. We gave Mr. Bush our note asking him for the sundae. Poor Mr. Bush was being lambasted with notes. We were not alone with our ice cream desires. His little drugstore had become full of girls with handwritten requests. I don't know which was worse for him—the noise or reading notes. Ruth and I went on about our enjoyment of this beautiful spring day by taking a lazy, leisurely walk. As Ruth stepped from the curb, a car suddenly appeared. I shouted, "Watch out!" Ruth stepped back, falling and saying, "Oh, no!" Yes, we both broke our silence. We didn't realize until it was too late that we could have received our pin because of the circumstances. Somehow neither one us cared. We were just happy to have it all behind us, though it surely was an experience I will never forget.

Easter was grand in every way, with sweets of all kinds as well as gorgeous flowers everywhere. The church celebrated Easter with glorious, powerful music which was exciting, but, oh my, the long line of people waiting for communion. I didn't think the service would ever end. For me, it was my squirming time, all of the while wondering what sort of an Easter Sylvia was having. I missed her this special day. She wouldn't have believed my weekend. It was indeed different.

The last month of school went very fast for me. Probably because of my dream, my vision of music was beginning to unfold. I was being asked to sing for so many different things. And the choir! How I loved it. I was happy, there was no doubt about it.

Tennis and spring was like strawberries and cream for me. Tennis had become an obsession. I laugh now, thinking it was a miracle that I didn't break my neck in order to grab the court before the other girls did. What a thrill it was receiving my basketball letter along with the upperclass. My grades, well, they were not the greatest, only average. Whoop-de-do! I more than expressed my delight of becoming a junior. I had arrived. I had not the slightest idea what I had arrived to, just that I had arrived!

Our first year at St. Helen's Hall had come to an end and Uncle Chet was waiting for us. And he was very pleased to see us until he saw all of our belongings—junk to him, but gold to us, every last drop of it. Uncle Chet grumbled while Sylvia and I chattered and carried on as though we hadn't seen one another in a million years. The two of us were in the same school, all right, but it was like we had been in two different worlds, so there was much to converse about. We were full of casual conversation, but it was exciting to us. I am sure Uncle Chet didn't miss a word of it, though he wouldn't have appeared interested if his life depended upon it. It wouldn't be right if he couldn't be just a little contrary. We learned very early that his bark was much worse than his bite ("Where is all of this stuff going?" Or, "You didn't start out with all of this baggage!"), so his words landed on deaf ears until we drove through the tiny town of Newberg and passed by a large, white structure. "Now, pay attention! This is the house where Hoover was born!" He never failed to remind us. From then on his mood changed.

How good it was to be home with Aunt Florence and Sugarpie. Of course, we both were eager to get in touch with all of our friends. However, I was disturbed to see that Aunt Florence's condition had worsened. She had been using a cane, but now she was depending a great deal upon a walker. I would never show my disappointment. Instead I bragged. "Gee, you do look great, Aunt Florence."

The first big event was Memorial Day. I hadn't forgotten about it, even though I had tried, yet there was something inside of me that was urging me to go. I was afraid that I would cry and make a spectacle of myself. "Girls, the Tillamook folks will all be here with their usual amount of flowers, so it wouldn't be right for us not to go. Not only that, but it is one of your uncle's favorite days. This is his time to be with his family, and with so many of his boyhood friends." I stiffened, knowing we should go. Down deep I did want to give Mother and Dad flowers. It would be so special, a flower just from me.

"Aunt Florence, I can't cry. But I'm so afraid that I will," I protested.

"What is wrong with tears?" she asked. "Heavens, I cry to this day when I am sad. Never be ashamed over a tear." I knew she was right. She always was, so I agreed to go.

We were warned about Uncle Roy: "He doesn't get around too well. Sometimes, he can't seem to control his walking. His legs go this way, and that way. We never know which way he intends to go. He even has gone backwards when he means to go forward. His arms resemble wings." Of course this didn't always happen, but if it did we were cautioned not to laugh because of embarrassment. I couldn't imagine Uncle Roy in such a condition, and I hoped it wouldn't happen this Memorial Day.

It was a gorgeous day—blue sky with ever so many white, fluffy clouds. *My angels*, I thought. And when I glanced over toward the old maple tree, I could almost see Grandma sitting beneath it with her famous apricot pie. Close by was Mother and Dad's neglected graves. "Oh, they do need flowers." I couldn't get a container of flowers fast enough. I carefully chose pink roses for Mother and then placed red flowers next to Dad's graveside flag. Cry? Oh, how I cried, and bit my lip till it bled. Ashamed? No, I really wasn't. I know that Mother and Dad knew...even though their graves were empty.

When our plot of the cemetery was finally beautifully decorated, the folks surveyed the situation and they all agreed, especially Aunt Ada who bragged, "Our graves are the prettiest up here."

"My Lord, Ada! Look what you have done!" Aunt Jessie said while laughing. We all observed, and much to our amazement, Aunt Ada had decorated her own grave.

"Jesus Christ!" she exclaimed. "Well, one thing about it, now I know what it will look like." We all went into a fit of hysterics. Even Uncle Chet laughed. I glanced over to where Uncle Roy was standing. Suddenly his feet were going forty miles an hour, but not making any progress at all. Then he took off like a big bird with his arms extended, resembling wings, but there was an obstacle preventing his line of direction. The roadblock just happened to be a bucket of water, which fit his foot perfectly. Aunt Jessie caught him, and Uncle Chet extracted his foot. Aunt Florence was so dumbfounded with Uncle Roy's antics, she nearly caused one of her own.

The folks had not had a picnic under the old maple tree since Grandma had died, so instead we had dinner at our place in Dallas. Not near as much fun, I thought, but at least the family was together. After all, this is what was important. The day was hard for the folks from Tillamook, it made a long day, so Aunt Ada was exhausted as she flopped into the nearest dining room chair. "Oh, I wonder if anyone would mind if I put my knees on the table," she said with a relaxed tone of voice.

"Yes, Ada, we would mind. Your elbows might be acceptable," Aunt Jessie corrected her while the rest of us hee-hawed. Uncle Chet had a skip in his steps and was in his glory bartending before dinner. When he asked Ada what her preference would be, I almost lost my cool when she replied, "Well, I guess I will have a monkey wrench. I do need something."

There was dead silence until Jessie piped up. "Ada, what in the Samhill is wrong with you? You must mean screwdriver." Again, our family relished in another very laughable shenanigan.

After Memorial Day, the Henkle reunion was to be the next big event. This was an occasion I never enjoyed. To me it was the bore of the year! Aunt Florence knew it, so with a chuckle and with tongue in cheek, she called to us. "Girls, are you ready for the big day?" We knew right off the bat what she was referring to. Sylvia nearly always got out of going, but I never did because Uncle Chet would have me scheduled a year in advance to sing during the program (beginning with this year). I was relieved to have Aunt Ada and Jessie going so I would have someone to sit with me. Aunt Florence felt it would be too much for her sitting on those hardwood chairs for hours. Listening to endless speeches would undo the patience of those who have the strongest of forbearance! And that was not me! My backside was positively numb.

Poor Aunt Ada, and Jessie wearing those uncomfortable corsets in the first place. How will either one of them be able to stand up? I wondered. Aunt Ada was so close to falling asleep when Aunt Jessie called my attention to her. "You better give Ada a nudge. She is going to break her neck, the way her head is nodding." So I poked her.

Just as I did that she jumped a foot, and shouted, "Mercy God!" her favorite expression. Believe me, our faces were red, but not Ada's. She had had enough of this business. I don't remember what song I sang that day, but I do know it was not a slow, lulling number. Instead it was lively, cheerful, and with much gusto. Uncle Chet, in his best suit and tie, sat next to the piano and close to me. He never had a compliment for me, only a half smile and an approving nod.

As long as my uncle was alive, I attended these reunions and the chairs were always as hard as ever and the speeches always the same, but for him, each meeting was more important than the year before. I appreciated later on in life as to how meaningful these people were to him. So many fabulous memories! I had to remind myself so many times that his parents, along with so many of these reunion people, were to-gether during a fabulous time of history—The Oregon Trail.

Morning tennis, afternoon swimming, and evening horseback riding with Pat; Cokes with the kids down at the town's favorite hang-out—What a neat summer! There were no dull times for me. I would feel guilty sometimes because I was having such a good time and my music was going very well for me. At least once a week I would be invited to sing for something, either at church, a lodge, or for a woman's club. What a nice experience for a growing girl, loving music. Aunt Florence was as happy for me as I was. She held such high hopes for me and my music. She was without a doubt my strongest supporter, so there were many precious sewing room visits regarding my dreams and ambitions. We would become excited together. What a glorious memory! She would speak of-ten about Sister Agatha Louise because of her interest in my voice. It would tickle me so much when she would say, "Now let's see, is she the fair-haired one?"

Trips? Yes, indeed! According to Uncle Chet, seeing the country was a important part of our education. This summer we traveled exten-sively through Oregon. There was Crater Lake and the Oregon Caves—so many beautiful, historical sections of our state. He didn't want Sylvia and me to miss a thing. Many times we would be exhausted! "Wake up and see the sights," or, "Step along now!" were his two very well-known phrases.

One of our best remembered trips was up into the Wallowa Moun-tains and Wallowa Lake, where we stayed for several days and had a marvelous time. Ivy went with us on this trip, as she had never before been there. Hell's Canyon was near there. Since Uncle Chet was deter-mined we take one day for this drive, it became a drive that none of us would ever forget. The road up the steep rough canyon was more like a dusty, narrow path instead of a road built for cars. "Oh, Chester, oh, Chester!" Aunt Florence was scared to death. I truly don't know what would have happened if we had met an oncoming car. We might still be up there. "This is crazy," Aunt Florence would say. It was very hot up there as we were in the eastern section of the state and it was the month of July. In those days air conditioned cars were almost unheard of, so we did suffer. None of us could stand it without a window open, which not only allowed the dust to blow in but also the grasshoppers. How the grasshoppers did adore us, especially Ivy's hat. She went into an absolute frenzy!

"Well, shut your window!" Uncle snapped. It was a wild ride. To give you an idea, the canyon is 6,500 feet deep with walls too steep to climb. They say a mountain goat might make it. It was an education and we stayed awake and we saw the sights. Believe me, it was breathtaking.

A good swim in that beautiful lake was an especially wonderful treat that night, one of the most refreshing swims I have ever experienced. Of course, what wouldn't be, after the trip we just had? Sylvia and I had fun teasing one another with every stroke we took. We had heard about a sea monster that was supposed to be living in the lake. Of course, it was nothing more than an old superstition, but it was fun anyway. I would yell back to her. "Sylvia, hurry up before you lose your toes!"

She would answer back, "You're the one who had better hurry because you are the one he is after!" Wallowa Lake was the favorite part of our vacation.

Before summer ended, I decided to spend a few days in Tillamook with Uncle Roy and Aunt Jessie to visit them and Ellna and take in the Tillamook Fair, which is always a reminder of the coming of fall. The folks were not too pleased about my going, but after so much pleading and teasing, they let me go. I also had several girlfriends living in Tillamook. I was excitedly making plans to go to the fair with them until boys became the center of their conversation. I felt as though I was completely out of their league. I had never been out with a boy, let alone having a boyfriend. "Oh, he is good-looking," or "Well, so and so had a car!" On and on they went while I foolishly felt insufficient and very immature. The girls would think I was from the backwoods, just a humdrum of a person.

There was a dance that night out at the fair grounds, and I wanted to go. Patty immediately invited me to join her and her date. She was sure her boyfriend could get me a date. He did just that. I had my first evening out with a boy. Now, of course, the negatives were really working overtime. *Maybe he will be short and fat. Oh, dear why am I doing this?* All kinds of worries were swishing through my mind. Patty assured me that

Ernie Hall was a very nice person and quite good-looking. I couldn't believe it when she said that he went to school at Hill Military. I suddenly became interested and excited. I flittered from one thing to another. Thank goodness I had calmed down a little by the time Patty, Chuck, and Ernie arrived for me. *I must not act bashful or timid!* I thought. I was pleased that he was tall and nice-looking and a year older than me, which I thought was good. Why, I don't know. He was easy to talk to, so this was a lifesaver because his dancing was nothing to rave about. He called walking around the dance floor dancing. I was glad when the dance was over and we were on our way home, even though I liked him. I liked him even more when he gave me my first kiss. My knees became weak and my heart thumped. I wished he would give me one more.

What a comedown to have to go back home and leave what I considered the love of my life, especially when Uncle Chet informed me that it was almost hop-picking time. He decided that I should find out what it was like to earn a dollar. "Pearl Hughes needs pickers, so you won't have a problem getting a job," he informed me.

Well, I wonder what this will be like? Right away, I called my girlfriend, Joan, and she was thrilled. "Just think of all of the money we will make." She was right, so we became anxious and excited about this new adventure.

Uncle Chet made certain that I was out of bed by 5:30 A.M., then satisfied himself that I ate a hearty breakfast by eating with me. He packed a man-sized lunch, even a banana for dessert. (In those days a banana was indeed special.) Joan came by our house because it was on the way to the hop fields. Joan was very fond of Uncle Chet, and this pleased me because so many of my friends didn't know exactly how to take him, and as ridiculous as it seems, adults as well as kids were weary of funeral directors. Joan was not. The last thing he said to us that morning was, "Don't forget to wear your hats."

We both said, "Okay, Uncle Chet." To this day, Joan still speaks of him as Uncle Chet.

Picking hops, we soon learned, was not fun and games. The first lesson I learned very quickly was how those hop vines would sting and burn your skin. That was why the experienced pickers kept their arms covered. We learned the hard way. The next day, Joan and I wore long-sleeved shirts without question. Hop vines grow on high wires and when a picker was ready for new vines, we were to call, "Line down!" A lineman would then bring down new vines filled with an abundance of hops. We both were too shy to yell, "Line down!" Standing there looking at Joan, I would say, "Aren't you going to call for the lineman?"

She replied by saying, "I thought *you* were going to yell." So we agreed with one another that we would take turns. Before long, we were yelling together. "My gosh, we are sure getting pushy and loud."

"Yeah, you would think we owned the place." We were getting pretty good, stripping the vines with our cotton gloves, and soon we learned to pick hops clean without getting leaves in our baskets. Boy! That sure hurt our feelings when the boss would bawl us out for picking dirty! We were grateful, too, for our straw hats. The old sun would get mighty hot during these early fall days. I will say one thing, we did have a glorious lunch break down on the river bank. Our breaks probably were the longest taken. It was a great experience picking hops. How proud we were of our first paycheck. I had many things planned to spend it on, but for some reason it took months to spend a nickel of it. I finally bought a pair of brown suede wedgy shoes. Believe me, I guarded them with my life.

It didn't seem possible that it was time to begin thinking of going back to school. Where had the summer gone? We were busy one day gathering up different things we didn't want to forget to pack for school when Paul dropped by. He didn't have anyone to do the music for a funeral and he was beside himself. Would Sylvia and I come to his rescue? Sure we would. Uncle Chet was out of town, so I knew how important this was for Paul. Sylvia had played the little chapel organ several times for kicks and we practiced a hymn together at home. We were all set for the funeral. No worry at all. I enjoyed helping Uncle Chet and Paul with arranging flowers. Even then I felt music and flowers go together, so if the truth be known, I was quite pleased to help this time with the music.

Sylvia and I were right on time the next day to help Paul. He was so pleasant as he escorted us back to the tiny room just off the main chapel with only a thin curtain separating the two rooms. Sylvia, appearing as though she was big time, sat erect at the organ while I held my hymn book with calmness. And oh! I was so very self-important. This organ, I'll swear, was one of a kind. Sylvia had to pump it with her feet, which reminded me of tapping the top of your head with one hand while making a circle on your tummy with the other. We both were doing okay in the beginning until a key stuck, which made a loud, bellowing sound, much like a donkey's hee-haw. We carried on. But wouldn't you know, this special note was all through the hymn. We couldn't escape it! Sylvia should have quit, as I could have carried on alone, but she didn't know this. As hard as we tried not to, we couldn't control those snickers. By the time the hymn finally came to an end, we both were in a state of hysterics. Even though we both were so sorry and, yes, ashamed! Paul was furious. He was so angry that he couldn't speak. His face became the color of a beet. I thought we were doomed for sure! But Paul, being the special person that he was, never did tell Uncle Chet. If he had, that old whale would have had a lovely time!

Chapter Sixteen

It was always wonderful to be back at school, and this time as a grown-up junior, but soon I learned it was nothing more than a continuation of being a freshman. I did have a new roommate, Harriet, who was a delight and full of mischief. Also Ernie Hall was now my boyfriend, which I thought was really a big deal because of his faithful telephone calls. He had permission to visit on Sunday afternoons, so now I gave the younger girls reason to spy. What goes around comes around, so I didn't dare complain. I was more involved than ever with my music and Mrs. Hilderbrant. She was working me harder than ever, but I was rewarded by singing solos frequently. My friends thought it was wonderful, and they always were there for encouragement and praise.

Because of Ernie, I always had an invitation to all of the Hill Military dances, which were fun except for dancing with Ernie. Much to my disgust, he still would ruin a good dance number by only walking. It always was a treat to dance with one of his friends. When our school had their dances, we had dance programs to fill out. This was perfect because my girlfriends would take up a good portion of my program with their partners. This little scheme worked out really well. Aunt Florence thought it was funny, but, of course, she would because she wished that I had never met him. We referred to Ernie's dancing as the "Ernie Walk."

Being sixteen and now a junior, I did have more privileges. I could go to downtown Portland without a chaperone. My emotions were stimulated to the limit my first Saturday out. I was going to lunch and to a movie with five of my best friends. All of that week we had been planning our big day. When our big day finally but most assuredly materialized, I could barely believe! There were the five of us sitting in a comfortable restaurant booth thinking how very suave and so experienced in the ways of the world we were. We were the cat's meow. That's what we were! When Hazel lit a cigarette, I was shocked. But then I thought again, *How sophisticated she looks.* And when Betty, a senior whom I had admired from the first day of school, took a gorgeous gold cigarette case from her bag and lit a cigarette, I was spellbound. I'm sure it was that lovely gold and rhinestone case that caught my eye more than the cigarette she smoked. She reminded me of a glamorous movie star. It seemed as though all of the girls smoked except me. It really never occurred to me to smoke. I hadn't given it a thought. But now, it seemed as though all of the girls smoked. Even my pal Pat had taken up smoking.

Before we left the restaurant, Hazel gave me one to try. She was about to light it with her fancy lighter when, lo and behold, Mrs. MacDonald appeared. She was one of the school chaperones. Here I was, stylish, and vain-glory with a cigarette in my hand, all ready for my first puff. I didn't have time to hide my wrongdoing, so I sat there shame-faced and embarrassed. I knew that I was in trouble. Mrs. MacDonald stared at me, expressing disbelief of that which she had just witnessed. She didn't say a word as she left, leaving me shaken and knowing that I was in trouble. *Why did I do this anyway?* I couldn't answer my own question. I had ruined my first day of freedom. I sat through the movie full of my disturbed feelings. The anticipation of the presence of Sister Margaret Helena, put me into an uncanny state of nerves.

That evening, Sister called all five of us to the parlor. There we were being lectured about cigarettes. We had disgraced the school and had broken the law, as well. "Don't you know that it is against the law for minors to smoke?" Sister reminded us. She punished us by taking our next Saturday privileges away from us. *Well, this isn't too bad,* I thought, and was relieved. But then Sister called to me and said. "Nadine, you of all people shouldn't smoke. Remember, your mother died of a lung disease. So keep this in mind. Not only that, but you could ruin your throat for singing too."

"Sister, I didn't even have that cigarette in my mouth," I told her.

"I guess Mrs. MacDonald probably saved you from a very sick experience," she said with a chuckle. And that was that.

Sister Agatha Louise still was depending upon my strong voice for her choir, so it was the same as last year. Mrs. Hilderbrant was still making sure that I knew the music. It was okay but sometimes I felt it was unfair, especially this particular choir practice. "Why do we have to have this dumb choir anyway?" one disgruntled girl said. The girls were grumbling and complaining like spoiled brats. In spite of the villainous attitude of some girls, the choir began on time with the booming authori-tative sound from the organ. Sister Agatha Louise began directing as if her life depended upon perfection. The girls sang as though they had one foot in the grave, with no enthusiasm whatsoever. So many times I would wonder, *What would happen if I hit a sour note? I think today will be the day.* So I hit the sourest note I could come up with and the girls fol-lowed! I have never seen so many startled faces before, including Sister's. The organist paused for a second, then continued on with Sister direct-ing. Practice continued with alertness and a tremendous amount of joy while she pretended nothing unusual happened. As we were leaving the chapel, Sister gently grabbed my arm. "Nadine, it was funny. But don't do it again!" Then she couldn't control herself. She laughed.

It was always exciting to go home for a weekend and this one was no different as far as excitement was concerned. However, it was different all right. After dinner, Aunt Florence said to me, "Nadine, your uncle wants to talk to you in the living room." Uncle Chet was standing in the middle of the room. *Now, what could this be all about?* I thought. *Maybe I am spending too much money on Saturdays.* I was completely baffled until I entered the living room.

"Here, take your pick. I have all of the brands of cigarettes lined up on the mantle," he said. I was one stunned girl when I saw, so neat and in order, in a perfect line...packages of cigarettes! They resembled soldiers ready to march in a parade. He was right, he had all of the brands, with Lucky Strikes leading the parade. I didn't know how to respond. I was scared, as he never before had had reason to reprehend me.

"I don't want them. Why not save them for Herman," I finally said. Then very easy, and in a soft manner, he gave me a serious talk about the dangers of cigarettes. Because he was so gentle about all of this, I couldn't help but cry while expressing how sorry I was. I was expecting a severe scolding and punishment.

Aunt Florence told me later that weekend it was the dark-haired sister who had written to them regarding my cigarette ordeal. I knew right away that she was referring to Sister Margaret Helena. Her beautiful brown eyes were a dead giveaway.

It was quite a weekend, but a good one. We nearly always went back to school with something new. Usually it would be an addition to our already beautiful wardrobe. Aunt Florence saw to it that we had the loveliest gowns for the dances and for my singing for programs or recitals. She made so many of our dresses, and believe me, they were elegant with her perfection. She would look so drawn with fatigue many times before we left for school because of the deadline she had to meet, but never did she express discontent. I worried about her and prayed that she would never have to be in a wheelchair.

Not thinking about herself, she had one more surprise to give: "How would you girls like to have ballet lessons?" I was filled with excitement like I had never before felt. A dream come true for me. I was in Seventh Heaven. I don't know how Sylvia felt about it, but for me, I couldn't get enough of it. Creating and expressing my sensitive feelings whether of sadness or joyfulness through dance is unexplainable. This was my most valuable gift from Aunt Florence.

She told me several years later that she had begged my father to give me ballet. He only would say, "I can't see a daughter of mine entertaining in such a cheap way."

"I think he thought of ballet dancing as being a vaudevillian act. Your poor father tried so hard and worried so much about you two girls," she said. She was very fond of my father and of his thoughts and feelings.

My junior year was a happy one, with many close friends to share good times and troubles with. Ruth, my closest friend, was a senior this year and this really had me concerned. I hated the thought of her leaving at the end of the year. I didn't dare dwell upon this concern. It was hard to imagine school without her. I would say that we were as close as sisters. It was so wonderful of Aunt Florence to insist that Ruth spend her weekends with us. Since her home in Alaska was so far away, our home became her weekend home. Of course, Uncle Chet was our faithful chauffeur from school. He never failed to slow down until we drove through Newberg! "Now, this is where Hoover was born." Being typical teenagers, this became extremely humorous, and it would have been a disappointment if he had neglected to point out this famous house. I'm quite sure he got a big kick out of our giggles; therefore, he never forgot his salute to Hoover as we drove through the tiny town.

What a marvelous year this had been, but before I knew it, it all had come to an end. Regardless of my dismayed feelings, Ruth was back in Alaska. We cried together before she left. *Why is life like this? Why can't we always be happy?* I believe all youngsters have these questions sometime during their growing years.

Summer was different this year because Aunt Florence's condition was much worse, to the point where she had to use a wheelchair. Traveling was difficult so she gave up taking long trips; however, we all enjoyed short vacations. Yes, my dearest Aunt Florence was in a wheelchair. She would say, "Why should I complain when I am not in pain and I have my mind?" Watching her struggle with this strange, crippling disease and yet never losing her enchanting, charming manner while always creating beauty has been a lifelong lesson of love.

Chapter Seventeen

My last year of high school was important in so many ways. Since music was still my love and passion, I became determined to make it my career. In the meantime, I was more than having a marvelous, fun time while only receiving average grades, which naturally I now regret. Ruth, my pal, was now attending the University of Washington, so it was a thrill for both of us to have her come to Portland and then go on to Dallas for weekends.

Ernie had graduated from Hill Military the year before, so the folks were hoping he would be going far away, perhaps to college. But he didn't. Instead he stayed in Portland and worked just enough to have spending money. He was always my date. Why? Out of habit, I guess: I couldn't stand the thought of hurting him.

Thanksgiving had come and gone, so now it was Christmas cantata planning. We were to meet in the auditorium with Sister Agatha Louise so she could announce her plans as to who would have which roll. I knew I was the only one for the angel Gabriel part, even though I was a brunette. (It was a rule that the angel Gabriel must be a senior and be blonde) I was wrong. I was in shock! So were the girls, as they stared at me in disbelief. Bea, the girl who was chosen for the roll, was a junior with long blonde hair. She had a nice voice but it was too soft for such a part. She, too, was not really happy about Sister's choice. Never before had a junior been chosen for this part, but Sister felt being a blonde was more important than being a senior. I was honored to have the roll of Mary, but I was sick at heart about having my beautiful dream crushed. It was difficult not to show my hurt, but it was so important to keep my dignity and pride. So with much fortitude, I succeeded in hiding my disappointment and hurt until lights were out. It was then that only God knew of my tears. Rehearsals began after dinner every night. They were not going well. The girls were lackadaisical and passive. Bea, with her sweet, soft crooning voice, could barely be heard. At first I could have cared less, but in time I became quite concerned regarding the cantata. Nothing about it was going right. After days of these limp, listless, so-called rehearsals, Sister Agatha Louise called and ordered me to the parlor. *If she thinks for one minute that these languorous rehearsals are my fault, she better think again,* I was thinking. So I was expressing haughtiness with every step I took. I was so sure that Sister was all set to rake me unjustly over the coals I walked with such briskness and speed that I nearly missed the parlor entrance. There she was, Sister Agatha Louise standing in the middle of the parlor brimming with love. I must admit the warmth of her smile melted my sizzling anger instantly. She reminded me of the cat who had just swallowed the canary. And I wondered what in the world was going on. Then she asked me, "Nadine, what on earth is wrong with you? You look as though you have just seen a ghost. Don't you know what is really wrong with the cantata rehearsals?"

I answered her by saying, "I felt the girls just didn't care anymore." Sister continued to tell me that the girls, including Bea, insisted that I was the only one to be the angel Gabriel." I have been the one who has made this serious mistake by thinking Gabriel had to be blonde. It is your voice we need, not the blonde hair. Will you please be the angel Gabriel this year?"

I couldn't speak without tears, not because I had received this favorite part of mine, but because of the girls' faith and respect for me. We only had a week left of rehearsals. But I will say that I have never before heard such singing. Yes, we were more than ready when the big night came and we sang with tons of enthusiasm. I wore my red robe and gold wings so proudly. When my gorgeous gold halo was placed with such loving care by Sister Agatha Louise, I felt as though there was a glow bracing me. And I promised I would sing like an angel!

When I glanced down into the crowded auditorium, my eyes were drawn upon a man in the front row. I was surprised when I recognized that this was my Uncle Chet. I was so thrilled that he cared I sang as though my heart would burst! The entire cantata was superb! As long as I live, I will never forget a darling little angel as she looked up at me with her big, blue, sparkling eyes and said, "I hope I can be the angel Gabriel when I grow up."

"I am sure that you will be if you want it bad enough." Then I had to chuckle to myself when I noticed what lovely blonde hair she had. The cantata was a big success this year and the sisters were all so happy about it, especially when both Oregon newspapers called it a brilliant spectacle, which pleased and delighted Aunt Florence.

Smoking, smoking! All of the girls were doing it except me. I felt like a ninny, and an oddball. I finally decided to do it. I justified myself by thinking that the folks just didn't understand! So the girls, especially Hazel, showed me how. Of course, they all about died laughing. I must have looked like Herman, I thought. I coughed and sputtered and went into fits of all kinds, but eventually I did learn at least the correct way of holding the cigarette and at least appeared as though I knew what I was doing. I thought I was really something! No longer was I an outsider. My next lesson was to learn the art of inhaling. Talk about sick! It was almost as bad as seasickness, but I kept at it until I was addicted, just like Aunt Florence said would happen. What a price to pay, just to feel included with my friends, even after all of the lecturing, especially from Uncle Chet. Most of my friends could smoke around their parents, but I had to hide my habit, though I am sure they knew. Being underage didn't matter at all because someone older would accommodate and buy our cigarettes for us. I am grateful that through my power of imagination I gave up this ridiculous habit. I pretended that I had never smoked. In other words, I brainwashed myself. Smoking to just be one of the gang was about the silliest thing I had ever done. I was already well thought of or I wouldn't have been elected president of the boarding department or chairman of several of the school dances and, of course, I was invited to sing over and over again for so many different programs. I had many wonderful friends and yet I did this dumb thing, thinking of myself as stylish and trendy.

Spring was wonderful to look forward to at the Hall—the thrilling, exciting formal dances, especially the prom, and now our Easter vacation. We all were allowed to go home this year, so there were no more silent days or long religious services to go through. I rather imagine it was more for the sisters' peace of mind. Whatever the reason, we did enjoy having an Easter vacation. It was a terrific pleasure, having Ruth travel down from Seattle to be with us at Easter time. It was during this time that Aunt Florence acknowledged that she and Uncle Chet wanted to adopt Sylvia and me. She wondered what I would think about it. I was startled at first, and then immediately said. "Aunt Florence, I already think of you as my mother, so it really doesn't matter if we are adopted or not."

She smiled happily with my response. "The rest of the family would be upset. This is why your uncle and I have been deliberating over this legal matter. They all have wanted you girls."

"You already have us, Aunt Florence."

Ruth was so touched by this tender, heartwarming conversation that her eyes filled with compassionate tears. "Nadine, what a joyful, happy Easter this one has become! Isn't it all so wonderful?" As her arm went around me she said, "And to think I could share it with you!"

I felt as though this spring was as beautiful and fresh as a new flower bursting open from a tiny bud, or as precious as a newborn lamb. It is no wonder that spring nearly always is the favorite of seasons. With spring came my beloved, exciting thrill of tennis. I nearly tore myself apart by rushing into a pair of shorts and tennis shoes, then speeding headlong (and in the nick of time) to be first! "Hurrah! I've got the court!"

"Wait a minute, Nadine," I heard someone call to me. "I want to talk to you for a minute."

I hope this is important, I thought, *because I am losing the court.* It was meaningful, indeed. It was the voice of Sister Margaret Helena, so I knew this must be a serious conversation because of the somber expression on her face and I noticed how hard it was for Sister to ask this question. But finally God gave her the courage. "Now, you can refuse doing what I am going to ask of you. And I will understand. You know that Mother's Day will be here in just a few days, so the sisters would be thrilled, so happy to have you sing in the parlor for our annual Mother's Day Tea." I was completely tongue-tied! And even though it was a very warm spring day, I shivered. I was frozen with puzzlement about myself. Would I be strong enough? Or would I become weak and cry? I would be so embarrassed! The only Mother's Day song I knew was the last song mother taught me. I loved it so much, *That Wonderful Mother of Mine*. Finally, I asked Sister if it would be all right if I could think about it for a little while. Of course, it was. So, forgetting my jolly time on the tennis court, I walked slowly and in deep thought back to my room. I sat at my desk in an absolute stunned state, trying to think! Mother and Mrs. Hilderbrant, as well, instructed, "Always sing to the one the song is about." *If I think of Mother, I'll break down for sure. But then,* I thought, *I have two mothers. One is gone, the other one is here. But both are in my heart.*

While all of this was going through my mind, Hazel came into my room. I was so tickled to see her because she is a good listener as well as a great talker. After listening to my scrambled emotions, she said very thoughtfully. "I wonder why your mother taught you to sing this song in the first place? I would think that she intended for you to sing it. I know that you can do it. I think it would be a shame if you don't."

So that Mother's Day, wearing the blue velvet gown trimmed in rhinestones which Aunt Florence made, I stood proudly by the gorgeous, antique grand piano and sang, *That Wonderful Mother of Mine,* all of the while thinking of my lovely Aunt Florence. I didn't have a tear, but Sister Margaret Helena did. Hazel, bless her heart, said, "You know, your gown just matched the blue in the parlor!" Hazel, my dear friend, was a marvelous conversationalist. The more she talked, the more excited she would become. All the while her right foot would twirl in a circle. A scatter rug didn't have a prayer. It would go around and around with her foot. Oftentimes a couple of the girls would put one foot each on the rug just to keep it on the floor. The excitement of this day wasn't any different for Hazel. It took several of us taking turns to keep the rug anchored.

St. Helen's Hall was humming like a hummingbird, as we were nearing graduation. So now more important decisions were to be made. College was the big one. I had not changed my mind regarding my singing and now dancing. The two went together for me, so I desperately wanted to choose a college of the arts. I had my eye on the Cornish College in Seattle. The sisters also thought it would be marvelous for me, but the more I thought about it, the more I changed my mind. I decided not to go so far away. I would miss Sylvia and the folks, so I selected the Hall's junior college, along with my friend Hazel. We would be roommates, so it was fun, all of our planning.

Before our baccalaureate service and the big night of graduation, there always came a special assembly with long speeches, school songs, good-byes, awards, and so on for the seniors. It seemed to me that we had been sitting there forever. My mind was miles away, wishing I could be out playing tennis. Anything would be better than this. All of a sudden, I felt Harriet give me a sharp nudge in the ribs. I almost fell off my chair when Harriet said, "Wake up! Your name has been called."

"Nadine Thomas, please come up front." I was more than just a little surprised and astonished. Shocked was more like it. *Don't forget to be calm and poised,* I kept telling myself, which was difficult to overcome under this unforeseen achievement. Whatever it might be, I had no idea.

Sister Superior smiled at me, knowing how deeply stunned I was. She was holding my award, which was a beautifully wrapped small box. Before presenting it to me, she had to tell her reasons for giving this honor to me. I was dumbfounded to learn the sisters had decided that I was the most outstanding girl of the boarding department, the girl who had made the most improvements. Then she read a list of my achievements. The small elegant gift was placed in my hand from her giving heart. The applause was overwhelming. Yes, I was thrilled, but also embarrassed. The gift was a sterling silver embossed spoon for candy and nuts. It was so beautiful that I decided the pattern (Reposite) would be my future sterling silver flatwear. Aunt Florence and her sister, Ivy, made this dream come true.

The baccalaureate and graduation services were as beautiful as ever. Both ceremonies were held in the huge, wondrous Episcopal Trinity Church. The baccalaureate service was the most impressive to see. Picture, if you will, forty girls clothed in immaculate, white graduation robes and waistlength, white chiffon veils, each girl carrying large bouquets of yellow roses and orchid sweet peas. We were spectacular while following the ornate gold cross down the long, bright red, carpeted aisle to our seating area. Uncle Chet and my two aunts from Tillamook were there for both services. You can bet your life they were seated in the front row for parents. I stepped along with my head held high while wishing Aunt Florence could be there.

Graduation night was notable and majestic—grand speeches and beautiful music. We were outstanding and stunning as well in our white graduation gowns and hats, especially in the shimmering candlelight which cast a beautiful, soft, feminine glow.

It was nice being home with Sylvia and sharing our room once again together. She was doing well, enjoying friends and school. Her piano lessons also were enjoyable. Her big achievement was swimming.

She had become an excellent swimmer. It wasn't any time at all when she became a member of the Multnomah swim team. This was so amazing to me, how she took to the indoor pool, as I detested it. It was the chlorine and the warm temperature of the water that always would give me a headache, but it surely was her cup of tea so this was marvelous for her. I loved bragging about my sister belonging to the Multnomah team! So now we were back home with so much to talk and laugh about. We would mentally revisit the Hall, and tell some of our funny happenings. I loved to tell the story about the night before lights were out when I had a surprise visit from Sister Superior. At the same time Ernie had strolled up to our iron fence and proceeded to whistle tune after tune, expecting me to come to the window. Sister carried on with her important conversation, completely ignoring the whistling. I was sure she was overstaying her visit. It seemed as though she would never leave. When she finally left, she remarked. "I do hope Ernie's lips get unpuckered." I was flabbergasted.

Sylvia's favorite episode was the night she and one of her friends raided the kitchen. They were caught, but she said it was so spooky, creeping around in the dark, that she would never do it again. That was punishment enough!

Sylvia's kitchen story reminded me of the deli feast several of us had planned. It was against the school rules to have food in the rooms, so we were really flirting with trouble, but naturally so intrigued. One by one we visited the delicatessen. It took hours to accomplish this feat because we had to smuggle the food in from underneath our blouses or sweaters—potato salad, ham, cheese, kosher dill pickles, and for dessert we had chocolate eclairs. Harriet was so funny. Because she was very short and quite buxom, she looked as though she was at least five months pregnant. I don't believe we were getting away with a thing. The sisters must have had a ball watching all of this. We stored all of the food inside of my bed. When it was time for bed, I perched myself up to the head of my bed and made a tent affair with my knees. Lo and behold, Sister Agatha Louise just happened to drop by for a chat. Where did she sit? Right at the foot of my bed, and right square on our potato salad. The aroma of garlic and onions was a dead giveaway, if she didn't already know. I was amazed that she didn't know she was sitting on some kind of a bump. Of course she did, and of course she could smell the garlic from the pickles! She must have been hysterical, inside. We were all bug-eyed until she left. (By the way, we ate every bite of the squished potato salad.) Nothing was ever said about our little episode. It was ignored completely. I figured the sisters had more fun than we did.

Our homecoming had a sad note along with our joy of being home. Our beloved little Sugarpie had to be put down just before our coming home. The folks told us that she was so sick and the doctor couldn't do anything for her, so she had to be put to sleep. Later I learned that she had been caught killing the neighbor's chicken. Losing a pet is devastating at any age, but especially for a child. I missed her so at bedtime, cuddling close to me or waiting so patiently under her favorite shrub for us to come home, regardless of time or weather. It took many weeks to get used to her not being there.

I was delighted to hear from Mary Hawke. She was going to be married in a few days and would I sing for her wedding? Of course, I was thrilled. It was to be a home wedding and I thought this would be wonderful. The Hawkes didn't live at the old farm anymore. Instead they had a new, smaller farm near Dallas. Uncle Chet took me to their home, but he would not go into the house. It was obvious that he didn't want anything to do with the Hawkes. I felt a little strange as I walked up to their front entrance. It had been so long since I had seen any of them, including Jean.

Nothing seemed the same. I missed the old house with its giant pine trees out front and, of course, my old friend Fritz. *But then,* I thought, *Fritz wouldn't like this place anyway.* The newness of the Hawke's new place seemed rather stark and cold. However, my feelings changed by the warm, affectionate greeting I received from the Hawke family. It was just like old times. After discussing my solo with the pianist and feeling somewhat at ease, I found a place to sit. As I looked up, I was surprised to see Albert Hawke sitting directly across from me. My heart jumped and beat a little faster. I wanted to ask him, "What did you do with Dad's will?" I tried to ignore him, but I could not! Every time I glanced in his direction, he would be staring at me. I then attempted to outstare this ugly, fat man with the slanted, tiny, squinted eyes, but he made it impossible. I had to get hold of myself, so I played my game, the one that I do so well. I would pretend that I did not know this man. When it came time for me to sing *Ave Maria,* I did it with all the love I could pour from my heart. Eunice and Jim were both in tears when I finished, so I felt my love touched the Hawkes. I sighed a sigh of relief, under my breath of course, when I had finished. Good! This man that I didn't know was still staring. The whale didn't make a fool of me!

Uncle Chet was waiting for me, but I decided to make him wait just a little longer as I wanted to enjoy a piece of Jean's wedding cake. Through my imagination, I did not recognize the fat man who complimented my *Ave Maria* solo. Uncle Chet and I drove back home almost in complete silence. There was definitely something between him and Albert Hawke. Whatever it was, my Uncle Chet did right, and that is all that matters.

Aunt Florence had been confined to the wheelchair for the past year. Even though she had seen many different doctors and received several of the latest treatments, including surgery, nothing was helping. Her crippling disease was a mystery. Even today multiple sclerosis is mysterious. We all were so concerned and worried; there was such a feeling of helplessness. I can remember saying to her, "Oh Aunt Florence, if only I had a magic wand." But none of us ever gave up hope, especially Aunt Florence. In the meantime, she had been reading about miracle cures happening at Soap Lake, Washington. People from all over the United States were traveling to this part of the country, expecting cures from arthritis to all sorts of skin diseases. Many doctors established their own clinics, luring patients to what they claimed to be miraculous healing. The chemicals from this lake brought about staggering, spectacular healings, so we believed it was worth a try. Uncle Chet agreed that the four of us should go to Soap Lake. We would never know if we didn't give it a try. Uncle Roy; Aunt Jessie; and their daughter, Ellna, joined us there.

I was amazed as to how hot and dry this part of the country was. I thought of it as a desert, and to see this large lake sitting in the middle of it was truly overwhelming. We were fascinated by watching the small waves at the edge of the lake. They were white with fluffy chemical suds resembling soap suds. I was excited, impatient, and bursting to jump into this weird, unnatural lake, with Sylvia running close behind. We didn't waste a minute...we were in the lake! Ellna stayed on the beach, feeling quite apprehensive. The lake was so heavy with chemicals that it was impossible to sink. Swimming underwater was hopeless. We tried to go under, only to pop back up as if we were maneuvered by a slingshot. Fun! Oh, such fun! We were overjoyed with enthusiastic laughter! I felt as though every muscle in my body was in a fit of joy. Many lake spectators, along with Ellna, were doubled up laughing at the outrageous show we were putting on.

The town of Soap Lake was unpretentious, with very few stores or restaurants. Of course, there were more clinics than anything else, and cabins for patients and tourists. I was intrigued by an entertainment center (hangout) for teens. I could hear inviting dance music playing as we walked by, so I dilly-dallied and took a sneak peek inside. It looked like fun in there and I wished I had someone to take me in. The center and the lake was just about it for kids.

Aunt Florence involved herself faithfully every morning taking treatments, as we all became overly observant and quite attentive to her condition, watching for some improvement.

Sylvia and I spent the majority of our time swimming and having a great time sunbathing, and a certain amount of horseplay. One afternoon our curiosity got the better of us. There was a nudist camp that we had to see for ourselves. Even though it was a very long distance away—clear across the lake—we knew we would be all right because we couldn't sink. So off we swam. It was tough going in this heavy water. I thought my arms would never be the same again. Finally we reached our designation, and when we did, several bare, browned persons stood up from their rock-circled hot beds to greet us. As they did so, Sylvia and I, in full tilt and as speedy as an arrow, headed for more familiar shores, completely forgetting about our aching, weary bodies. Uncle Chet welcomed us as we dragged ourselves from the water. We did not slump or waver, instead we stepped along and held our heads just as high as he did. Not a word was spoken. However, there were thoughts. He had told us before, "Now, you kids stay on this side of the lake." I am sure he was wondering what we had seen. We weren't about to tell him.

Time was going fast for all of us. I couldn't believe there were only three days left of this very different fun kind of a vacation. We were sorry for Aunt Florence though—she hadn't made any improvements. But she did appear more relaxed and rested, so that was good. I couldn't understand how Uncle Roy could drink so much of this awful-tasting mineral water. He could make several trips a day uptown to the water fountain. I would have to hold my nose just to watch him swallow that nasty, smelly liquid. He never batted an eye!

It was amazing, the suntans Sylvia and I attained in only two days without burning. We both were as dark as if we from the Middle East. It had to be from the chemicals that were in the lake. Wait till the kids see us at home. They would be so jealous of our tans!

After much encouragement from Aunt Florence, Ellna and I decided to please her and spend an evening up at the kids' hangout. I really didn't know what to expect, but whatever I was thinking, I was surprised to see so many young people having such a glorious, swinging good time. The kids all had their own tables with soft drinks or ice cream, so Ellna and I found a table of our own and ordered a Coke. With much interest, we proceeded to enjoy watching couples dance. I became very fascinated with one special young man. I was certain that he must be a professional dancer by the style and elegant way he moved. I had never seen anyone dance this smooth and smart before, except in the movies. Ellna, holding her breath, whispered to me, "Have you ever seen anyone dance like he does? And he is so handsome." I was so deeply engrossed by this young man everything else was a blur. Even when he left the dance floor to relax with friends, my eyes were still glued on him. Ellna was talking, but I didn't hear a word. The next thing I knew his eyes were fixed upon me and we began staring at one another. When the music began to play again, I found my hand in his, and we were dancing together. We danced as though we had always been dancing together. We were falling in love without a word spoken, there was no doubt about it. I was wishing that this night would never end. When the music ended, we made our own by humming together and we danced up and down the sidewalk. Ellna had gone back to our cabin quite disgruntled, so we had the rest of the wee hours to talk and learn about one another. He was just two days older than me, since his birthday was February first and mine the third. We both had just missed Groundhog Day, so we laughed.

With that gorgeous, auburn, curly hair and laughing blue eyes, it was quite obvious he was Irish. I loved his name, Riley. He was such a ray of sunshine. His father was a builder, so he worked for him, but he was wishing that he could go on to college. I was sorry for him. Building houses at this time was just a little slow. I told him that he should go to Hollywood because he was so handsome and talented. He walked me back to our cabin. We kissed and kissed again, not wanting to say good night. As I remember, it was daylight.

The next two days we were together almost constantly. Aunt Jessie also was quite taken with him. She said, "I'll tell you young lady, if I were near your age I'd have given you a wild race for this young man." Riley could put a spell on most everyone, not just by his looks, but by that radiant personality as well. Our last night together was an impossible night for dancing, we were too heartbroken. So we walked and walked most of the entire night, almost in complete silence. Finally, we sat down in the sand close to the water of the lake. The quiet of the night and the soothing, rustling sound of those white, fluffy waves gave each of us a comfortable feeling. Riley spoke to me as though he had just seen the light. "Okay, everything is going to be all right!" We both began to talk. We talked about our future, how exciting it all sounded. But just the same, when it came time to say good night, we cried like two babies. He held me so close, it hurt. But I didn't care.

The drive home from Soap Lake, naturally, was not as exciting or as full of anticipation as going. I was too sad leaving Riley and dreading my encounter with Ernie, which was only a few days away. We were to meet in Tillamook for the Tillamook Fair. The folks made sure that I wouldn't miss the fair, as they were elated that my breakup with him was right around the corner. Aunt Florence wasn't fooling me in the slightest. She had a reason for giving me all of that delightful freedom in Soap Lake.

Chapter Eighteen

I knew how pleased the folks were that I was breaking up with Ernie, but still they were understanding and sensitive to my emotional feelings. Uncle Chet went with me to Tillamook. That night, when Ernie came for me, he was so thrilled to see me and to show off his new car! He bought it especially for me. I wondered, *How am I ever going to tell him?* He had decided that we should take a drive up the coast before going on to the fair. *Well, that is fine,* I thought, except it was an extremely dark night, much darker than usual. (It can do that over on the coast.) I felt nervous inside, a quivery feeling, as though someone was trying to tell me something. I said, "Ernie, it is so dark we won't be able to see a thing. It is a bad night for a ride."

He ignored me, and drove on. "I want you to see how nice the car rides, then we will go back to the fair."

We already had driven several miles up and around the narrow, winding, seemingly endless curves. "Your car, Ernie, does really well. So why don't we go back now?"

We were almost to Neahahnie Mountain when Ernie said. "I only received two letters from you while you were gone." I thought right away that this was the time to break the news to him. I had to get it over with, so I told him as gently as I could. "I knew the minute that I saw you that something was wrong," he said. He began to sob and shout at me. He went berserk! He whipped the car around and headed back toward Tillamook. Down and around one curve after another, he was yelling horrible, vicious accusations at me the entire time. He must have wanted to kill us, because he refused to use the brake. I have no idea how fast we were going. Even though my eyes were closed, I could hear the screeching, almost screaming noise from his tires. I was aware of the white guardrail between us and the rugged surf below. He must have come to his senses as we began to come closer to Tillamook and into the traffic, because now he began using his brake.

There was such a strange, eerie sensation that came over me while we were coming down from the mountain. I didn't have a tear, a scream, or a tremble. I felt as though I had been drugged, or perhaps all of this was just a terrifying dream. It was almost as though none of this was happening. It took several days, however, to put Ernie's stinging words and that haunting screeching noise out of my head. There were no good-byes of any kind as he left me in front of Uncle Roy's house. I raced as fast as I could to my room, as it would have been intolerable for me to have to face the folks. They came home from somewhere, soon after I did, and it wasn't from the fair. I have always had a hunch that they knew what had taken place. Until now, I have never told another person about this horrifying experience. I still think so much of Ernie. Hurting him has been a difficult thing for me to live with. Yes, I escaped the whale, but not without a hurtful scar.

I was happy the next morning as Uncle Chet and I were preparing to go back home. I was thinking how wonderful it was to have such a happy home to go to. I was so very grateful that my understanding family never once mentioned Ernie's name.

Before we left for the car, I noticed Uncle Roy still had jugs of Soap Lake water sitting on the porch. Uncle Chet said, "Yeah, he has been trying to give me a jug of that rotten stuff." We both had a good chuckle as we were leaving.

Aunt Florence was eagerly waiting for our return home, especially for me. "Look here!" she shouted, while waving a letter in front of me—my first letter from Riley! I held it as if it was my most precious treasure. It was all that I had hoped it would be.

There I was in college. It was almost more than I could believe, but exciting, and for Hazel, my roommate, as well. Of course, we were full of chatter because of the many thrilling, stirring events between the two of us. When Sister Margaret Helena came into our room with a beautiful vase of red roses, the entire dorm went into orbit. They were for me from Ernie, wishing me good luck in my first year in college! I wished that he had not done this. I must have expressed my feelings because Sister Margaret Helena more than reprehended me for such unappreciative attitude. I could only think, *She just doesn't know.*

School was okay, but my heart really wasn't with it. I knew it was because of Riley. I not only missed him, but my heart was longing for him. Even my music was taking a back seat. The challenge and thrill of a song had left me. Riley had been just as miserable. Much to my amazement, Riley came to Portland that fall! I was beside myself with overflowing joy and amorousness for this beauteous young man. I was in complete surprise, as I didn't expect to see him until spring. The drive from eastern Washington to Portland, even today, is considered a difficult trip with hard driving, so back in '39, it was even more so. When the winter weather arrives, it indeed becomes hazardous and dangerous.

We resembled two small children manifesting their charm for Christmas. We were bubbling with enthusiasm and passion for one another. He would grab me, and hold me as though he feared I would slip away. Many times I would express discomfort: "I can't breath." But then

I would think, *I do like feeling as though I am a part of him.*

I had a delightful time showing him several of Portland's out-standing attractions. Washington Park, with its spectacular rose gardens, was a must. The gardens were still gorgeous this fall. I was pleased as to how he enjoyed the beauty and the luscious aroma of the roses. I was more in love with him than ever. He must have felt the same way, as his arms went around me and he began humming *Star Dust* softly. We danced to our humming, as we did in Soap Lake, only this time we danced along the brick paths, between the beds of roses, up and down the terraced steps, effortlessly. We were so in love and intrigued with one another that we were completely unaware we had attracted an audience not until we heard clapping and one man shouted at us, "I'll bet that was *Star Dust!*"

Riley called back, "You are right. Now guess what this is!" He hummed the *Beer Barrel Polka*. We took off like the wind. The man did guess. Oh, what fun we had. In no time at all, our weekend was gone. You couldn't even call it a weekend, we only had the one day. And by the time we shared dinner together, it was time for me to be back in school. Riley left bright and early the next morning for home. It was difficult never being able to be alone, but still we were so thrilled to just be together.

Winter arrived in spite of our feelings. With a stiff upper lip and determination, I began to adjust my life back on track. I kept myself extremely busy with my music and each day I became more and more interested in my ballet. Mrs. Hilderbrant allowed me to use the dance studio anytime it wasn't occupied, so I took advantage of this wonderful opportunity. I relished in this strenuous output of physical and mental concentration. The beauty I felt filled my mind and spirit with pleasure and loveliness. Dancing gave me an inner release, as had swimming years earlier in my lake.

I wouldn't be seeing Riley for several months, and since Ernie wasn't around anymore, boys were beginning to ask me for dates. I didn't feel right accepting, not until the girls, especially Hazel, encouraged me to go out. "Good heavens, you can still be true to Riley," they would say. I was glad that I did because I was privileged to take part and enjoy this beautiful age of the Big Bands. I had the thrill of dancing to both of the Dorsey bands, Phil Harris, Glenn Miller, and countless others. The Big Bands would come to Portland and also to the dance halls over on the coast. It was a wonderful time to be alive!

One evening, while home from school, Pat and I were uptown enjoying a Coke at the old hangout. She was going to Oregon State, so we had lots to talk about. While we were talking up a storm, Jay, an old friend of ours, slid into our booth. He was a popular young man in Dallas but I was not at all fond of him. He was the one who delighted in scaring me with garter snakes and stinging my legs with navy beans when we were little kids. I always stayed clear of him. When he sat down with us, I decided to excuse myself and leave for home. As I did so, he said, "I'll be happy to take you home."

Pat said, "Go ahead, I'll see you tomorrow."

Well, there wasn't much I could about it. On the way home, he said, "You are the one, I'm sure, who broke up with Ernie,"

"I don't know what difference it should make to you, but yes, I did the breaking up," I answered.

"But even so, you must miss his lovemaking," Jay said. I was dumbfounded. He parked his car and continued to talk about Ernie. He had known Ernie in the past. Then this egotistical young man was all over me! He was a big guy, and strong.

"Jay, please take me home," I ordered him, but he completely ignored me and continued to force himself on me.

"You won't miss Ernie any longer," he kept saying while attempting to undo my clothing. I socked him a good one when he managed to get on top of me. I thought that if I had to, I would bite. Well he ended up with a bit lip and a bruised face.

"What a mess Jay's face is," Pat informed me the next day. I was still pretty shook up, but I was more concerned about having my favorite blouse ruined; however, I felt lucky I came out of the ordeal unscathed. I later heard Jay had told the story around Dallas completely opposite of what had happened. My reputation had been falsely smeared. I prayed that the folks wouldn't hear the lies. My instinctive dislike and fear of this person was right. I guess we all have to learn the hard way.

Riley made the trip back down to Portland that spring and we were as crazy as ever about one another. I wanted to sneak away and get married. We almost did. Riley, thank the Lord, used better judgment. He wanted everything absolutely perfect for us—big church wedding, exotic honeymoon, and money in the bank. I knew he was right, so we more than had exciting, wonderful plans. As I think back, I now realize what a strong young man he was for only being nineteen. Financially, he was on his own. Just that last year he came to Portland in a beautiful new car. He always wore tailor-made suits, the best of everything. He never seemed to be lacking in any way. He treated me like a princess. Our marriage was to be perfect, but it wouldn't be for a year or so.

I had decided not to return to junior college the next year, so I began once again pestering and almost begging Uncle Chet's permission to attend Cornish School of the Arts the next year. "Absolutely not!" he said. Finally, giving up, I agreed with him to go over to Monmouth to college. It was a nice, small college, quite close to Dallas. I am sure that his main concern was having me close to home. He thought, too, that I would make an excellent teacher—Monmouth was a teacher's school. Emma Henkle was a professor there. Not only was she a cousin, but a close friend of Uncle Chet's. "He sure trusts me, doesn't he," I said to Aunt Florence.

"Your uncle trusts you. Nadine. He just doesn't want you to go so far away. His main concern is that he wants you to get a fine education." That was the end of that conversation. Once Uncle Chet made up his mind about something, that was it! No ifs, ands, or buts about it! I could have one tantrum after another and it would only make him more stubborn than ever.

It was frustrating, and yes, sad for both Riley and me to never have any privacy of our own. It was especially hard for Riley, after traveling such a long way, to only have a short day, or maybe two, with me. One time, whether it was right or not, I said to Riley, "I do believe with all of my heart and in God's eyes we are married." He didn't say a word for a long while. "Are you ashamed of me for thinking what I am?" I asked him.

He was stunned. "You want to stay overnight with me, don't you?"

"Well, we could go over to the coast and get a place to stay. No one will ever know. I even know of a tiny chapel where we could pray together about this. It is right on the way, you know, Riley, we don't have to sleep together to be together," I said convincingly.

Finally he said, "Okay, let's do it. We deserve more time together." He was becoming excited and really glad about what we were planning.

I had checked out of school, packed, and was all ready for the coast. We took off with a song in our hearts. At last we were going to have some time to ourselves...precious time! I couldn't believe what a beautiful, sunny Saturday afternoon we had been blessed with. We couldn't have ordered a more perfect day if we had tried. Our trip to the coast was a gift from heaven. But first, Riley and I had to keep our promise to visit the tiny Episcopal chapel. We did this kneeling so close together in silence and with sincereness. We talked with God.

I enjoyed watching the expression on Riley's face when he first set eyes upon the powerful energy of our beautiful Pacific Ocean. He appeared to be paralyzed by the superior beauty of it. The long stretches of clean, sandy beach were overwhelming. We walked and walked most of the afternoon, saying very little. How mystical a kiss can be while standing on the warm sand, feeling the ocean's soft, moist, breeze about our faces, giving us a sense of veritable paradise.

It was significant, and as luck would have it, Bob Crosby's "Bob Cats" were to play at the Logs dance hall. Riley and I were ecstatic. We danced that night until I thought my legs would never be the same again. The aches and pains left when the band played *The Big Noise of Wenucca*. We were so elated and stimulated with this animated dance number that we heard nothing but the beat of this rousing number. What a thrill! What sheer joy! We felt as though we were in a world all of our own. In one respect we were. Much to our surprise, the dance floor had cleared and we were dancing alone. For how long, I don't know. There was applause! I was embarrassed and Riley appeared bashful and quite demure. He managed a shy smile. We gracefully left for our motel. I thought I would be in a state of self-consciousness being alone with Riley, but instead I was calm and composed. Riley's emotion was one of strong, masculine passion. We didn't hesitate from making gentle, heavenly love.

Riley made several trips to Portland that spring and much to my dislike and lack of understanding as to why, he was becoming such a show-off in front of my friends. I even criticized him for it. "Please, Riley, don't act like such a clown. It is so unnecessary." He only laughed, but I wasn't laughing. He was embarrassing me. I couldn't help having my feelings flip around and change. This worried me. I didn't want to lose my precious love for him. I kept telling myself that he soon would realize what he was doing. We nearly always would go to a Saturday night dance when he would came to Dallas or Portland. And, of course, my friends would invariably ask me to dance. Riley would never give his consent. At first I thought this was kind of neat. (My ego, I guess.) But it didn't take long for me to resent it. Of course, some of my dearest, old friends were puzzled and somewhat stunned.

Ruth and I corresponded often with one another. Several times during the year she still would spend weekends with us in Dallas. This was one of those special weekends, as it was nearing the time when she would be returning to Fairbanks.

We were having a good time, as we always did, with so much to talk about—her life in Seattle, naturally my decisions regarding change of college, and of course, my problems with Riley. "Sounds to me that he is very jealous and this will surely lead to trouble. Bad, bad business. You think you have troubles now. Just wait till later!" she kept saying.

I kept wondering, *How could I be so in love with someone and then be almost completely afraid of that person.* "I know the time is coming when I will have to break up with him. But not just yet," I said.

Before the day ended I was called to the phone. I had the surprise of my life. I was so surprised that I nearly dropped the phone when the male voice announced himself as Larry Bennett. He wanted to take me out the very next evening! My heart was in my throat. I couldn't believe what I was hearing. He also had a date for Ruth. I was beside myself with emotions stimulated beyond disbelief. I began running up and down the stairs, shouting! "I don't believe it! I don't believe!"

You don't believe what?" Aunt Florence asked. She had never seen me so wild. "You are acting crazy. You had better calm down. Whoever this is will think he is going out with a maniac."

"Aunt Florence, I have been in love with this man all of my life, but I thought he had dropped out of existence. I thought he had left the country."

Aunt Florence was pleasantly shocked when she discovered who I was talking about. She was very fond of Larry and his family. Larry had been away for some time at a college in California. I had been too shy to inquire about him. I even imagined that he could be married and even have a family. Wouldn't he laugh, though, if he had known that I had been singing love songs to him for years! No one knew but God and me.

Leave it to Ruth: "Nadine, what about Riley?"

I couldn't answer her, but I did say, "Ruth, I don't know about Riley." Nothing more was said about my serious problem. Right now, I was so excited and filling myself up with so many negatives, I almost became ill! What would I say to him? Would I look like a kid? I went on and on, scaring myself silly. The closer the time came for our evening out, the paler I became.

"For heaven's sake, girl! He wouldn't ask you out if he wasn't interested." Aunt Florence was becoming disgusted with me.

"Well, I don't see why he would be interested in me in the first place!"

"Oh go sit in Grandma's chair and get yourself quieted down. And don't sit down in a foolhardy way, either." Aunt Florence didn't know what to do with me. I sat in Grandma's chair and gently rocked.

"Okay Grandma, help me out. I am so scared that he won't like me." I did get help from somewhere, that is for sure. It was marvelous for me when he and his friend arrived. My butterflies turned into thrilling little flutters. He was as I remembered—very handsome with a serene confidence about him. It was so special, the warm friendliness he expressed for Aunt Florence. I felt at ease and comfortable, as if we had known one another for years. Strange as it seems, we had never been introduced. We four had a delightful evening but, of course, it went too fast. He was gone like a puff of smoke. I was disheartened that there were no letters or correspondence of any kind. I thought, "That's that!" and went on about my way, but not so merry, and not in such a carefree way.

I was a fortunate young girl because I always had a date to go with to the Big Band dances during the summer and always had a partner for morning tennis. Pat and I had wonderful times horseback riding in the evenings. The only activity I had that wasn't frolicsome or sporty was my music. I religiously settled down every day in front of the piano with a serious determined attitude. I demanded excellence for myself. Every day, before I began practicing, I could always count on Aunt Florence calling out to me, "I want to hear *Over the Rainbow*." I never was quite sure if she wanted to hear the song for herself, or for me. But I was sure of one thing, it was her favorite song and I loved singing it every day.

The thought came to me one day that I shouldn't just do things that only I enjoyed. I should have a summer job, like so many of the other kids had. The more I thought about it, the more I liked the idea. Since a new Ben Franklin store had just come to Dallas, I almost broke my neck getting my application in to them. Hurrah! I got a job clerking. I don't think I have ever been so proud! My first job! The folks were so pleased for me. I was doing a good job when six older boys walked into the store and began singing *I Saw a Million Dollar Baby.* I was so unnerved and shocked that I might as well have gone home. The lady manager politely asked the boys to leave. Not a word was said to me. Later, however, she came to see Aunt Florence and explained to her about the boys and their song and why she felt that she must let me go. She didn't want the folks to think that I hadn't done a good job. She knew she must hire a girl who needed the work. My summer job sure didn't last very long.

I didn't see Riley during the summer because this was the big season for building. We were still writing, however, but not as often. I knew our romance was almost over. It was just a matter of time.

Larry came home from California, but he was busy in a nearby town with a part-time job in a law firm. He dated me several times during late summer. Just being with him was special. I can truly say that he was the most important man in my life, but it was curious and odd, as in the beginning he left without any correspondence at all. I always wondered if I would ever see him again.

Just before I was to leave for school, I was invited to sing a solo for the First Christian Church. I was happy to oblige, so I sang, feeling grateful for the privilege of doing so. A young man was my accompanist, which I was not aware of until he called the next day. His name was Hugh Springsteen. I had to leave him dangling on the phone long enough to find out who he was. "Who is Hugh Springsteen?"

Aunt Florence answered, "He is a very nice young man. Quite a musician, I'm told." Aunt Florence would know. I went on a date with him and our entire evening was a treat, talking with someone who had the same ambition and dreams. He was a singer, a baritone, and in a few days he was to leave for the Chicago School of Music. Naturally, I was impressed.

Chapter Nineteen

There I was in college! A new school for me. Even though it was a small college, it was big and lonely for me. I missed my sister. Already, I was homesick. I kept telling myself to shape up! *This is ridiculous. You are only a few miles from home. What if you were clear up in Seattle? Well, we won't think about that, will we!* It didn't take long, thank goodness, to become adjusted and acquainted with so many girls who eventually became my good friends.

I was presently surprised about my new voice teacher. She not only was a marvelous teacher, but also was an accomplished concert contralto. I felt very fortunate to have her. I was also pleased to find so many other music educational courses that were interesting. What I did not expect was the fabulous dance program! So far, I was thrilled with everything. Mrs. Marvel, the voice instructor, took a great deal of interest and time with me. She scheduled programs for me to sing, and also for school assemblies. This was such fun for me, as well as being good for me. Not only was I becoming well known on campus for my vocal talent, but also for my love of dance. To share my emotions, especially my happiness, through dance was the most glorious feeling there was. Sometimes I would think my heart would burst!

One of me dearest memories took place in the girls' dorm before final exams. We were all hitting the books like fury, becoming more tense and crabby by the minute. Finally, as it was nearing midnight, we gave up the books and, feeling what I call slap happy, I turned our radio sound up to a great jazz program. I grabbed my red satin Chinese robe and put on a crazy, gray, straw-brimmed hat which had a large bunch of daffodils sitting on the brim. They resembled a coal miner's headlight. Off I went, lickety split, with a carpet sweeper as my partner into a jazzy, sexy dance. Up and down the dorm hall the girls turned the jazz program up as loud as it would go. They went crazy, clapping and laughing with merriment! I was scolded by the dorm matron; however, she didn't have her heart in it. I knew it all was well worth the minor criticism!

Mrs. Marvel organized a girls' sextet. I was pleased to be selected as the soprano. We were plenty good, which was a popular, big success for the school. We sang everything from the *Lord's Prayer* to the then popular *Three Little Fishies in the Itty Bitty Pool.* Our experiences were wild at times, and hilarious. Then there were those heartwarming, dear times.

I was enjoying everything about this school and the beauty of the campus. It was wonderful to see students with so much respect and esteem for their school. Everyone could feel the appreciation we all had for the old, ivy-covered structures and the beautiful old trees shading the deep green lawns. Because of the admiration and pride of the students, there was no litter.

Emma Henkle, who I resented in the beginning, had become a delight. Many evenings I would find her wandering to my room for a chat. Yes, we became friends, but I felt sorry for her, as well. She told me that when she was my age she was deeply in love and they were planning on being married, but her parents insisted that they needed her more than her sweetheart did. "Now, don't you make that mistake! Don't end up being an old maid like me!" I was not surprised when she spilled the beans about Uncle Chet. "Let me tell you, he was a wild one. If you think he is strict, just remember he is well aware as to what is out there!" We always had a good laugh before she left my room.

I was satisfied with my average grades, lucky to do that well since most of my time was spent singing or dancing...my passion! Riley arrived later that fall. I was thrilled to see him. The girls all went gah-gah when they saw him. "Wow, what a looker." There was no doubt about it, he was as gorgeous as ever! His visit was a more pleasant one this time because he wasn't the show-off that he had been. He seemed different, somehow. He appeared older and quieter, which was unusual for him. I became quite puzzled while watching him read an article from our school paper. It was a write-up about me and a ballet number I had done. The article referred to me as "the beautiful Nadine." I was surprised when he didn't respond or show any interest at all. I thought he would be proud of me, but there was only a troubled, concerned expression about his handsome face. He finally smiled, but his smile lacked sincerity. One girlfriend said to me, and I did think about it, "Remember, Nadine. He knew you while you were in a girls' school. Now it is altogether different."

I went on about my life with loads of enthusiasm. I loved everything that I was doing. There was fun everywhere. The school dances were sheer joy, nothing but happiness for me. I never sat out a dance. It was so wonderful to always have a partner. Emma laughed, saying, "Give me a little of that energy, will you?"

I was pleased, and felt quite honored to be elected chairperson of the spring formal dance, the foxiest dance of the year. I was gung-ho about this affair. It would be flawless! That was, and is, me—a perfectionist! The best local band member who I could think of was over in Dallas. That weekend I would go home and see if I could locate him. I found him okay and I didn't have any problem making an appointment. I was elated. While I was meeting with him, Riley had driven down unexpectedly. Of course, I had checked out at school, so he drove on over to Dallas. Aunt Florence was startled and bewildered to see Riley standing out on the front porch. She could only say that she didn't know where I was, only that I was out on school business and she didn't have the slightest idea when I would be home. Poor Aunt Florence was so upset, she waited up for me until I arrived home. "You can't guess what! Riley is here staying at the Dallas Hotel, so you better hurry over there!"

Of course, Uncle Chet said, "Let him wait until morning!" Ignoring my uncle, I rushed to the old wreck of a hotel and found a very angry Riley. No way did he believe my story about the dance band, so it wasn't a very pleasant weekend. I was disturbed because he hadn't let me know that he was driving down. "You were just checking up on me," I said, which he obviously was. (By the way, I did get the band to play for our spring formal and it was great music. The spring formal was as beautiful as I had hoped. Everyone had a marvelous time, including myself.)

I had been receiving letters from Hugh which I thoroughly enjoyed because of our music interests. There was not, however, any romantic feelings. It was all music. The folks were concerned about Riley. "I can see that Riley has a real Irish temper. It is a worry!" Aunt Florence would say. I eased her mind by telling her that I had written just to tell him that right now I only want to concentrate upon my music. This was several days earlier and I hadn't heard from him since. It hurt me, because I had loved him with all of my heart and soul. It wasn't until Larry popped back into my life that I knew. I know, too, that Riley sensed it. "Don't you worry about a thing." She couldn't help but be concerned about Riley. He could become dangerous. However, she chuckled about the music career. "Oh, you wait till Mr. Right shows up," she said more than just once.

I continued to stay home for the weekend when my friend Martha Jean came over to join me. It was like old times. We went out to a movie and then for a bite to eat. Who should be sitting near our table but Larry and a lady friend of his. I'll bet I turned every shade of green there was. I was jealous. I was so full of jealousy that Martha Jean couldn't stand it and she went home. "Nadine, what is wrong with you?"

"Larry was out with another girl. She wasn't even a girl. She was an old lady!" I shouted.

Aunt Florence was more than just a little disgusted. "Heavens, you go with whomever you want, why can't Larry?"

"Well, I didn't think about that." I said.

Aunt Florence gave me quite a lecture. "Don't let jealousy come into your beautiful life. It is the ugliest emotion there is and that is the fastest way to lose your beauty." I can honestly say that she couldn't have taught me a better lesson. Many times I have had a little twinge of it, but I can get rid of it just as fast. I have often wondered how a victim of jealousy copes. It can be just as painful.

We were having a school program and it was being presented this lovely spring evening. Our sextet was to sing several different numbers. We were all spiffed up in our attractive powder blue uniforms doing our thing, when I glanced to the rear of auditorium. Who should be standing near the exit but Larry and a friend of his. I was so thrilled at first, but then I thought, *He just knows that I will drop everything and go out with him, as that is what I have always done.* After the program was over, I did go for a drive with him. I was cool toward him. He recognized immediately that things were different. He felt there was someone else, and I allowed him to think so, hurting him. There should have been more communication between us. I was spoiled by so much attention from the boys at school. Larry would show up at the slightest provocation unannounced, and after long lapses of time. I felt in time he would break my heart.

Summer was different this year, except I was still teasing and arguing with Uncle Chet to allow me to go next year to the Cornish School in Seattle. Mrs. Marvel agreed with the sisters that this would be wonderful for me. There were so few music courses left for me at my present college. Uncle Chet was a very stubborn man, and I was just as headstrong, making home a rather tense place to be. Hugh was home from Chicago for the summer and had a summer job. Since I was still studying voice for the summer with Mrs. Marvel, he decided to study under her also. He felt good about her, as I did. We were seeing one another almost every evening. Several times I would attempt to get together with Pat and my other girlfriends, but something always seemed to interfere and I would end up with Hugh. Mrs. Marvel decided it would be a fine idea if Hugh and I would give a recital in Dallas, so this we did. We worked hard. On the other hand, it was a wonderful experience for both of us and it was fun also. The recital was given at the Christian Church on a Sunday evening. The church was packed with interested musicians but mostly by friends and Dallas acquaintances. Uncle Chet was in the front row! Hugh looked handsome in his tuxedo. Sylvia and Aunt Florence thought I was gorgeous in my white taffeta gown which had the fullest of skirts. I know that I was in my glory, ready to sing. I was wishing Larry were there. He had never heard me sing. After the recital was over, I heard many times, "What a handsome couple you and Hugh make." Hugh had become in love with me, but I was torn. I knew he had become a close friend to me because of our music, but I wasn't at all sure that this was love. I wished we were not together so much. I thought it was a little strange that Hugh's mother not once complimented me after the recital. Maybe she just forgot to.

Now, Uncle Chet made a compromise with me—not as far as Seattle, but I could go to Portland and study voice once again with Mrs. Hilderbrant.

142

I had a small cute apartment in Portland that I shared with another girl. I also took a few courses at Portland State (music). A new opera company had come to Portland that was a branch of the San Francisco Opera Association. I now became a part of the opera. I was all set. Mrs. Hilderbrant was pleased about the arrangement. Her apartment was my place for practice. This was to be an exciting year for me. The folks, however, were disheartened when they learned that Hugh was also planning to go to Portland. I, too, was surprised with his decision, but it was okay. He would be working during the day and I would see him during opera rehearsals and that would be about it. It all would work out fine. I would enjoy being closer to Sylvia. I tried out for the choir at St. Stephen's Cathedral and was placed in the soprano section. I felt that the more experience I could get, the better I would become. I learned a great deal from this extremely knowledgeable master choir director. I loved it when this slightly plump, very English man would make a booming sound from the organ and then rear back and shout, "Now make a joyful noise!" He enjoyed me also because of my range. Several times he put me over into the alto section. Perhaps he felt it would be a challenge for me, or maybe he was just curious. Whatever, I had a good time.

Chapter Twenty

December 7, 1941. We were at war with Japan. Hugh and I were coming from church when the news hit the media and fell upon our disbelieving ears. My first reaction was, "It must be a mistake." But of course it wasn't. Who would ever want to destroy our beautiful country? There was not one American life that wasn't affected in some way. We not only were at war with Japan, but we were on our way to Europe, as well. I had no feelings at all. I guess this is what people mean when they say, "I am numb." Our family had a personal worry at this time because our Uncle Chet was in Hawaii with the Willamette University's football team. As you know, it was Pearl Harbor in Hawaii that was bombed. He arrived home okay after traveling in the bottom of a blacked-out ship for three weeks. Bless his heart, he came home with two treasures—our grass skirts! We never heard one word regarding his trip home. It must have been a gruesome experience. Aunt Florence said one day, "Chester will not talk about his journey at all."

The National Guard boys from Dallas were sent to the South Pacific almost immediately, boys who were good friends of ours, young men with whom we had grown up.

I knew that we must think about our lives as to what was important right now. Hugh definitely had decided to enlist in the Navy. He was worrying about leaving me and was talking about marriage. I was not thinking about my feelings but was more concerned with his. After all, he was the one who was going off to war. He was a good person who had ambition and loved me. Also, he would be a good father. I knew all of this, so what more could I want? I could make him happy, and what was more important than happiness right now? That is the way I was thinking. We decided to get married in a few weeks. Aunt Florence and Uncle Chet did not argue with me about our plans, but it was obvious that they were not pleased. Aunt Florence wasn't well at the time and leaving the house was difficult for her. We planned a small home wedding for her sake. My good friend Pat showed her displeasure by saying, "Nadine, my mother wants me to warn you about Hugh's mother. She really is not a nice person and might make your life a living hell!" I couldn't believe it. So we went along with our original plans. Even if Pat was right, I was sure I could handle the problem. Pat and her mother gave me a charming bridal shower, even though she was fearful for me. The church also gave me a large shower. It was so wonderful of them to include my mother's close friends from Sheridan, which was a complete surprise for me. This was a wonderful time for me. My wedding-to-be was becoming exciting.

The day of my wedding, I became quite nervous even though everything was pretty and all of my friends were happy. Aunt Florence had the house just perfect. My gown was beautiful. Sylvia was adorable in her dusty rose formal. When I decided to go downstairs for something, I found Aunt Florence crying. I was stunned. "Aunt Florence, aren't you happy for me?" I asked her.

"I was thinking, you will never dance again. How can you be happy?" she cried. (Hugh didn't dance at all because it was against his mother's religious beliefs.) "Dancing is such a part of you," she still was crying.

"I'll get around it, Aunt Florence, don't you worry," I said, hoping I made her feel better. I felt troubled inside just the same. No one ever knew how close I came to not going down those stairs to my wedding. But I did! My new name became Mrs. Springsteen. Our honeymoon didn't amount to much because of the war. I cried most of our first night together, but coming back to Portland and to our lovely apartment was exciting. I loved keeping house and making things look pretty. Cooking, well...the only thing I could make was applesauce and macaroni and cheese! It was Uncle Chet who had taught me this. I had much to learn, but was enjoying it all. I had my own money for music. I was still studying and I might add I was working hard at it. Hugh never knew from one day to the next when he might be called to duty with the Navy, but we didn't allow ourselves to dwell on it.

Only a month had passed when I discovered that I was pregnant. I was high with the greatest thrill of my life! Hugh seemed pleased, but no one was more tickled about all of this than Sylvia. She was so cute, planning right along with me. I remembered that Dr. Martin (his daughter attended the Hall) was considered the best obstetrician in Portland. I remembered what Dad always said, "It is always less expensive to go to the best." He was to be my doctor. I felt fortunate to have a doctor who wasn't a complete stranger. After he made himself known to me, he said, "Oh, you are the girl who has the beautiful voice." He couldn't have said anything that would have pleased me more or have put me more at ease. He had heard me sing at one of the Hall's programs. We got along famously. I felt as though I had a fatherly friend as well as a good doctor. It was difficult for me to give the needed medical history of my family to him. I knew it would shock him. "Well, young lady," he said. "You have a hell of a beautiful future coming." I couldn't help but chuckle, hoping he was right.

I do believe that I sang more and better during my pregnancy. I had never been so happy, that is, when I wasn't throwing up. I had my share of morning sickness.

I was in my third month of pregnancy when Mrs. Hilderbrant informed me that she had registered me to sing for the Day Music Company recital. I was to sing *None but the Lonely Heart* and Deanna Dubin's *A Heart That's Free*. Always pleased to perform, I wouldn't dream of refusing. I laugh now thinking how Sylvia and I struggled to get my once tiny waist zipped up into my formal gown. Sylvia was all eyes. Little did she know that she would be going through this five different times herself someday! How uncomfortable I was sitting there in that tight gown. And, wouldn't you know, I was the last one to sing. I almost forgot my composure. But as soon as the gorgeous music of *None but the Lonely Heart* began, I felt the beauty of it from the tip of my toes to the top of my head. The thrill of the music came pouring through me, gladdening hearts and bringing tears. The music seemed to draw people from the hotel, and passersby flocked to the music room to listen, as though the music was magic.

Mrs. Hilderbrant, with a joyous smile, said, "You made your music glow! You lifted spirits!" There were tears in her eyes. Then came the big surprise: I was overwhelmed to be confronted by three different men. One was from the First Baptist Church of Portland. He offered me the soloist position for the church! The second man was from the largest department store in Portland. He wanted me to consider doing special holiday music for their tea room. Last, but not least, would I come to radio station K.G.W. for an interview?

At first, all of this just had not soaked in, not until the next day. And then, I was overflowing with excitement. *Won't it be wonderful to have that extra money?* I thought. I was beside myself. Hugh didn't express himself one way or the other and, to stop and think about it, he didn't have one word of praise. I didn't know what to think. His being quiet grew worse and then I was given the silent treatment. I became so upset I couldn't eat. I tried, but nothing would go down. I wanted to go home, but I could never do that.

Aunt Florence sent me a letter addressed to Nadine Thomas. I couldn't imagine what this could be. It was from a Marine buddy of Riley's. He explained that he got my address from one of my letters to Riley. He went on to tell me that Riley had been killed in the South Pacific. He always had my letters with him. I was ill from this shock. Gorgeous, vivacious Riley! How could he be gone? He was such a beautiful part of my life. The memories of him were so dear, so precious!

I didn't do well at my next visit to Dr. Martin. He said, "What is going on here? You are supposed to be gaining weight. You have lost." I felt like a fool, but I couldn't help it. I broke down in tears, as I said, "I can't sing anymore. My husband, I guess, doesn't want me to sing." I told him all about the recital and my wonderful offers.

Dr. Martin didn't speak for some time. Then he said, "Things have a way of working themselves out. My concern is for you and your baby. It sounds to me that your husband has a touch of jealousy. Or maybe he fears he may lose you. Just put it all out of your mind. You will see, things will be all right. This baby of yours will be the most important treasure of your life. I suggest you begin to express music in other ways. You can do it." I felt so much better after my visit, so much better that I made a visit to the soda fountain and treated myself to a huge milk shake. When Hugh came home that night. I was surprised he was talking. I imagine that Dr. Martin had something to do with it. Whatever happened, it was plenty nice. We even had a good laugh over my weird dinner. I looked right straight into Hugh's eyes and said, "There is music everywhere. Listen! We can hear it now."

What about the whale? Well, I can take anything he can dish out!